What people are saying about *Conscious Capitalism* . . .

"Superb research and writing! David Schwerin presents a very readable and convincing plea for bringing spiritual values to bear on our challenging economic and social problems." —**George Starcher,** Secretary General, European Baha'i Business Forum

"When someone from the financial sector writes about business with a conscience, sit up and read! When you share his sweeping view of all the road signs of where humankind has been, should be, and where it is today, it's time to get excited about the new consciousness that is taking hold—even in business." —**Perry Pascarella,** author/speaker/former publishing industry executive

"No one is more qualified to combine money issues with ancient wisdom than businessman and esotericist David Schwerin. And no one writes about these two fields with such clarity and insight, drawing from an astonishing range of disciplines and thinkers. If you want to know how joining business and Hermetic Principles can create a revolution in humanity's e⋯ ⁴⁻⋅·work and thought— and have a great read while you're at it—this book is for you." —**Denise Breton** and **Christopher Largent,** authors, *The Soul of Economies; The Paradigm Conspiracy;* and *Love, Soul, and Freedom*

"David Schwerin has written an inspired, practical, and sensible exposition of ageless wisdom principles for the contemporary business leader. Speaking from the front lines of high-stakes business experience, he illuminates the causes of persistent business dysfunctions and failures. This book is a big part of the solution." —**Robert Rabbin,** author, *Radical Agenda: Practical Mysticism for the New Leaders;* coauthor, *The Values Workbook*

"*Conscious Capitalism* makes good economic, business, and social sense. Schwerin offers a compelling prescription for how unfulfilled people can attain personal growth in the workplace in a way which is good for their companies and their professions." —**John White,** author, *What Is Enlightenment?* and *The Meeting of Science and Spirit*

"David Schwerin delivers a revolutionary business guide that shows how to create the success of the future from the ancient wisdom of the past. Required reading for every business leader who wants to stay at the cutting edge!" —**Rosemary Ellen Guiley,** author, *The Renaissance of Soul in the Workplace*

"David Schwerin's documentation of the evolution of capitalism from competition to cooperation matches well the progression from individual appraisal to team awards. Excellent in describing the underlying principle driving the awareness of interconnectedness." —**Werner R. Olle,** retired Manager, Lucent Technologies, Inc.

"David Schwerin masterfully brings together the worlds of ancient wisdom and modern commerce in a way that informs, inspires, and helps to create a future we can all look forward to. This is a wonderful book!" —**John E. Renesch,** editor, *Leadership in a New Era: Visionary Approaches to the Biggest Crisis of Our Time;* co-editor, *The New Bottom Line: Bringing Heart and Soul to Business;* editor, *The New Leaders* newsletter

"David Schwerin helps us managers come to terms with what we've always known on some inner level—people thrive in mentoring environments, and mentoring environments encourage excellence from the top down." —**Meredith L. Young-Sowers,** Director, The Stillpoint Institute, Walpole, New Hampshire

"A wonderful description of various holistic approaches to business . . . reinforces the concept that healthy relationships with our environment, other human beings, and other businesses is what makes the modern business successful." —**Joel Levitan,** CFO, Kripalu Yoga Fellowship

"This is a business book with a difference for those who are seeking answers to the changes taking place in our socioeconomic structures. It is a fascinating treatise which should leave no reader unaffected." —**Geoffrey C. Thomas,** retired Director, General Motors Acceptance Corporation; Chairman, GMAC Mortgage Corporation

"David Schwerin has written a brilliant analytical book which should make all business executives rethink their mode of operation and plans for their future careers. Leaders in highly-charged business positions need to step back from time to time to reexamine who they are and where they are going. Dr. Schwerin provides a valuable guide for this all-important appraisal." —**Arlin M. Adams,** retired Judge, United States Court of Appeals

"Conscious Capitalism is an exceptional integration of business principles with the universal principles of ageless wisdom. David Schwerin illustrates what a vital role business will play in humanity's transition to align with the creativity, vitality, and adaptability that lies at the heart of the human spirit." —**Angeles Arrien,** Ph.D. Cultural Anthropologist, author of *The Four-Fold Way* and *Signs of Life*

"Conscious Capitalism draws on the world's wisdom to picture a more humane way of doing business. This is our chief task in the next decade—to bring soul to public life—and David Schwerin has made a remarkable, thoughtful, and helpful contribution." —**Thomas Moore,** author of *Care of the Soul* and *The Soul of Sex*

CONSCIOUS CAPITALISM

CONSCIOUS CAPITALISM
Principles for Prosperity

DAVID A. SCHWERIN, PH.D.

BUTTERWORTH
HEINEMANN

Boston   Oxford   Johannesburg   Melbourne   New Delhi   Singapore

Butterworth–Heinemann supports the efforts of American Forests and the Global ReLeaf program in its campaign for the betterment of trees, forests, and our environment.

Library of Congress Cataloging-in-Publication Data

Schwerin, David A., 1942–
    Conscious capitalism : principles for prosperity / David A. Schwerin.
       p.   cm.
    Includes bibliographical references and index.
    ISBN 0-7506-7021-5 (alk. paper)
    1. Industrial management—Psychological aspects.
2. Entrepreneurship—Psychological aspects.   3. Industrial management—Moral and ethical aspects.   4. Entrepreneurship—Moral and ethical aspects.   5. Social responsibility of business.
6. Executive ability.   7. Self-perception.   8. Self-actualization (Psychology) I. Title.
HD31.S3425   1998
658.4′092—DC21

                                       98-10854
                                           CIP

British Library Cataloguing-in-Publication Data

A catalogue record for this book is available from the British Library.

The publisher offers special discounts on bulk orders of this book. For information, please contact:
Manager of Special Sales
Butterworth–Heinemann
225 Wildwood Avenue
Woburn, MA 01801-2041
Tel: 781-904-2500
Fax: 781-904-2620

For information on all Butterworth–Heinemann books available, contact our World Wide Web home page at: http://www.bh.com

10 9 8 7 6 5 4 3 2 1

Transferred to Digital Printing 2006

This book is dedicated to my wife, Joan, for her selfless support of this project and all my endeavors. No one could ask for a more talented, devoted, or loving partner.

Contents

Preface

When I first met Hermes—Hermes Trismegistus or Hermes Thrice Great—he evoked more questions than answers. This legendary figure told me, as he has told all seekers of truth for ages, that soul searching introspection, when pursued long enough, leads to intuitive breakthroughs. After more than a decade of study I now see how this nonsectarian, scientifically based, ancient body of knowledge has direct relevance to modern day business.

For over thirty years I have experienced the ups and downs of the turbulent world of business. My career in investments and finance together with outside interests have allowed me to observe people from all walks of life—powerful corporate executives, steel-hardened prisoners, penniless Cambodian refugees, influential investment bankers. Managing a small business I have experienced all the pressures associated with soliciting and retaining clients, the difficulties of overseeing a staff of diverse personalities, the aggravation of negotiating with money hungry service providers and the frustrations of dealing with counterproductive regulatory requirements. I have dealt with the emotional traumas of those recently widowed and divorced and have had to learn how to interact with extremely wealthy individuals, a few a bit pompous, most exceedingly gracious. My work and my spiritual searching have been a great aid to my slowly evolving comprehension of the cosmic puzzle. Why are we here? What are we supposed to be doing?

This, then, is a book about how a business career has helped me come closer to that ever-elusive quest for self-knowledge. It stems from my deep desire to tie together what has occupied most of my time for the past three decades; my work and my interest in understanding the secrets of the universe. While this may seem like an esoteric and lofty pursuit, the chapters are grounded in "real life" issues regularly faced by companies around the globe. As we delve together into ancient wisdom, money and commerce, scientific facts and metaphysical philosophy, magical keys may unlock solutions to your own vexing business problems and lead the way to highly practical applications.

Over the years Hermes has given me many profound insights, but, whatever the subject, he always emphasized the following point:

> The possession of Knowledge, unless accompanied by a manifestation and expression in Action, is like the hoarding of precious metals—a vain and foolish thing. Knowledge, like Wealth, is intended for Use.[1]

I invite you to join me in discovering the gems contained in Hermes' teachings and then, by all means, let us put them into practice.

NOTE

1. Three Initiates, *The Kybalion* (Chicago: The Yogi Publication Society, 1912), p. 213.

Acknowledgments

As a result of writing this book, I have discovered at least one subtle connection between Hermes and me. As Hermes was considered thrice great, I consider myself thrice blessed, by a loving family, wonderful friends and inspiring guidance. While it is not possible to name them all, I wish to acknowledge those individuals who played a major role in *Conscious Capitalism* from conception to culmination.

My mother has always been a source of nurturing and support. I thank her for her enduring love and concern. My son, Eric, brings indescribable joy to my life and love to my heart. He is a vital source of wisdom and understanding and I consult him eagerly and often. My sister, mother-in-law and sister-in-law have all played an invaluable part in helping me understand myself better. Their caring natures have been excellent models for me to emulate.

Barbara Good, Ph.D., is a true friend, always able to find the proper balance between enthusiastic encouragement and constructive criticism. Her efforts and skills played a crucial role in the development of this book. Pat Fenske, Ph.D., is a terrific mentor and teacher. Whenever I needed assistance she was always willing to oblige. Arnie and Rebecca Shapiro's wise counsel and readiness to help, no matter what the task, are sincerely appreciated. Everyone needs friends like the two of them. Chris Largent and Denise Breton have always provided valuable advice and encouragement. They are a font of knowledge for which I am most thankful. My longtime friend, Bruce Topman, has assisted me in a variety of ways. I greatly admire the conscientious, disciplined and skillful way he approaches all his endeavors. Bob Bobrow made it much easier for me to write this book and earn a living at the same time. He can always be counted on to lend a helping hand.

Donna Evans Strauss, Ph.D., has played an indispensable role in all aspects of this book. I consider her inspiration and guidance gifts from on high for which I am eternally grateful. Builders of the Adytum's teachings and lessons are a phenomenal repository of ancient wisdom without which I could not have written this book. I am indebted to those who keep this knowledge alive. My father and brother, as well as the others in the invisible world of spirit, have helped me in more ways than I can possibly imagine. You are always there when I need help and I hope you are collecting time and a half for all your overtime. Finally to Hermes, wholehearted thanks for your continuing insights and inspiration. A few more lifetimes and maybe I will be able to comprehend fully the marvelous treasures you have left humanity.

1

Self-Discovery at Work

Today we find ourselves in a paradoxical situation. We enjoy
all the achievements of modern civilization that have made our
physical existence on this earth easier in so many important ways.
Yet we do not know exactly what to do with ourselves, where
to turn. . . . There appear to be no integrating forces, no unified
meaning, no true inner understanding of phenomena in our
experience of the world. . . . The abyss between the rational and
the spiritual, the external and the internal, the objective and the
subjective, the technical and the moral, the universal and the
unique constantly grows deeper.

. . . VACLAV HAVEL, President of Czech Republic[1]

I have been fairly successful in my career, my three children are
"launched" and have begun their lives, and my marriage is
satisfying. Nevertheless, I'm unhappy and it feels like something
is missing. To be honest, I'm embarrassed to admit having these
feelings because I don't feel I should have them.

. . . Anonymous fifty-five-year-old man[2]

Over the past decade, while many businesses have pursued what
I call business as usual, I have been part of a different, smaller
business movement—one that has tried to put idealism back on
the agenda. . . . The New Corporate Responsibility is as complex

as changing our basic notions of what motivates us as business people, of what our basic corporate goals should be. This shocks many people: they think it is a radical idea to consider anything other than financial profit. . . . We, as business leaders, can and must change our views and our values.

. . . ANITA RODDICK, President, The Body Shop International plc[3]

These three quotes—from a philosopher/statesman, an introspective United States citizen and a trendsetting British businesswoman—represent the thoughts and feelings of a vast cross section of humanity. The authors hail from three different countries and have all reached a point in their lives where they should be able to analyze their experiences with a good measure of insight and objectivity. Their sentiments are reflective of two seemingly unrelated, broad-based movements that have been proceeding on a parallel course. Each appears destined to make an indelible mark on society at large. The first movement encompasses those individuals who are earnestly searching for greater meaning in their lives. There are clear indications that this includes an ever-increasing part of the population. According to an article written by pollster George Gallup: "There is a great deal of evidence that Americans are beginning to break their secular chains, that we are, indeed, in a period of spiritual renewal."[4] The second transformation is taking place in the business world, in particular among those companies which are undertaking a thorough examination of their priorities, mission and values. On the surface these movements appear unconnected. As will be shown in subsequent chapters, these trends are very much interrelated and tend to reinforce one another.

The urge to find greater meaning is evident throughout the popular culture. A look at the nonfiction best-seller list reveals a growing interest in books on spirituality and related material. From "everything you ever wanted to know about angels," to an ever-expanding variety of books on "new age" thinking, most bookstores are devoting increasing space to these subjects. Barnes & Noble and Borders, the two largest bookstore chains in the United States, now offer yoga demonstrations, tarot card readings, lectures on massage techniques, all-day sessions on holistic synergy and reflexology and visits by hypnotherapists.[5] Motion pictures frequently deal with topics such as past lives and near-death experiences. America's Public Broadcasting Service (PBS) has found that guests such as John Bradshaw (humanistic psychology), Huston Smith (world's religions) and Joseph Campbell (mythology) have attracted enthusiastic audiences. A number of Bill Moyers' PBS programs have covered arcane topics that were not part of the vernacular until quite recently. Based upon a recent poll, 48 percent of Americans say astrology is probably or certainly valid. The number of professional astrologers in the United States is estimated to be around 5,000 versus 1,000 just 20 years ago and the annual market for astrology books has increased fourfold during the past three decades.[6] From this short survey of popular culture, it appears that many people are willing and, in fact, eager to explore new ways of looking at the world and their place in it. They are, in essence, hungering for self-knowledge so that they can understand the age old mysteries of "Who am I?", "Where have I been?" and "Where am I going?" In other words, "What is life all about?"

The same gnawing dissatisfaction, frustration and, in many cases, insecurity that has led people to search for deeper answers in their personal lives has encouraged business leaders to look for more productive and fulfilling ways to structure their organizations. In some cases survival itself has been the motivation; in other instances, progressive business leaders understand that meaningful changes are necessary if both their enterprises and the communities upon which they are dependent are to prosper. With the mind-boggling pace of technological change and the intense competition generated by the globalization of markets, businesses feel pressured to downsize, outsource and generally rethink the optimization of their resources and relationships. A complex regulatory environment, a more diverse and family sensitive work force and an ecologically vigilant consumer add to the pressure to re-examine all business practices. Under close scrutiny many of the old ways of thinking and behaving are ineffective in solving today's problems. A broader vision and new style of leadership is required. The former requires a much longer-term perspective, while the latter needs to be based more on a leader's heart and soul than on behavior or authority. Primary emphasis is shifting to the human element from the previous focus on monetary and physical assets. In our fast-paced world, the success of a business enterprise now depends on the active collaboration and contribution of creative, well-trained, motivated and dedicated employees.

A significant amount of research points to pervasive feelings of confusion and discontent throughout society, both at home and in the workplace. There is simply an insufficient connection between our daily activities and our purpose for being. While not a new phenomenon, constant feelings of consternation and dissatisfaction are becoming intolerable to a growing number of people. According to a *Business Week* article subtitled "Can spirituality enlighten the bottom line?" those employees who have survived downsizing and re-engineering are asking themselves, "What is going on?" and "Why do I feel so unfulfilled?" The article responds: "A growing number of companies are setting off on spiritual journeys . . . the spirituality movement in the corporation is an attempt to create a sense of meaning and purpose at work and a connection between the company and its people." The authors discuss the fact that AT&T has referred hundreds of middle managers to Transpective Business Consulting where, at a grueling three-day course, participants are helped to be more effective leaders by turning inward. Aerospace giant Boeing hired poet David Whyte to speak to five hundred top managers three days a month to help bring to life the experience and emotion of change. Says Whyte: "All the companies that are alive are realizing that they need more creative, vital and adaptable workers. All that creativity and vitality and adaptability resides in the soul." One senior executive, who was initially skeptical, now concedes that Whyte: "Helped us to think differently than we ever had before. We had to look inside ourselves."[7]

Some critics believe that blending spiritual and business interests is like combining oil and water; they do not mix. One is concerned with pragmatic affairs and the other with ephemeral matters. Internationally recognized investment pioneer, Sir John Templeton, emphatically refutes this notion: "I think all careers are more successful and satisfying if you use spiritual principles. I can't think of a single exception."[8] Mahatma Gandhi, one of the most inspirational and effective leaders of the twentieth century, concurs with Templeton's assessment:

> If any action of mine claimed to be spiritual is proved to be unpracticable it must be pronounced to be a failure. I do believe that the most spiritual act is the most practical in the true sense of the term.[9]

It is the contention of this book that a complete reversal of many long held values and beliefs is a prerequisite for attaining the peace and contentment that is earnestly sought by citizens throughout the world. Preconditions for such a reversal are already in place. In fact, the fundamental building blocks upon which to base a "new" world view have always been with us; they are an integral part of "ageless wisdom." Ageless wisdom is one of several designations given to a certain body of knowledge that is neither affected by the passage of time nor is the product of human thought. This same knowledge—rooted in the unchanging depths of the universe—has been termed "forgotten truth" by Huston Smith[10] and was referred to as the "perennial philosophy" by Aldous Huxley. According to Huxley, this wisdom can be found among the traditional lore of aboriginal peoples in all regions of the world and, in its more developed form, has a place in the teachings of most sacred traditions.[11] Author John White seconds this view:

> The perennial wisdom is unchanging; truth is one. That is agreed upon by the sages of all major religions and sacred traditions, all

hermetic philosophies, genuine mystery schools and higher occult paths.[12]

One of the most ancient codifications of ageless wisdom is attributed to the widely revered Hermes. While details of his life are lost to history, it is said he lived in Egypt and was a contemporary of Abraham. He was deified under the name Thoth in Egypt, and appeared in the Greek pantheon as Hermes and later, in the Roman tradition, as Mercury. Hermes stature was such that he was considered a messenger of the gods. Among men he became the patron of merchants, and the god of eloquence, good fortune and prudence.[13] Given these attributes, Hermes would surely be an extraordinarily valuable advisor to any company's board of directors.

Ageless wisdom, in all its variations, is a distillation of the experience of many inner explorers over thousands of years. What they discovered is that God is one, whole and undivided, encompassing and interpenetrating everything that is. A central tenet of the perennial philosophy is that all of humanity can become consciously aware of this infinite and eternal wholeness. Indeed, the wise tell us that it is man's single highest need and desire.[14] As emphatically declared in Hermes' famous Emerald Tablet: "That which is above is as that which is below, and that which is below is as that which is above." The familiar, six-pointed Star of David, composed of two overlapping equilateral triangles, one pointed up and the other pointed down, is said to symbolize this profound statement. Put another way, everything is of the same essence; it is the task of human beings to remember their divine origins and reorganize their lives so that what is below once again mirrors what is above.

KNOW ONE, KNOW ALL

This seemingly Herculean feat is facilitated by becoming more conscious of who we are as we go about our daily activities both at home and at work. Knowing ourselves better leads to a fundamental change in the way we think about our personal and social relationships, how we interact with the environment and, ultimately, how intimate a connection we establish with God. A traditional Islamic saying makes this point very succinctly: "Learn to know thyself. Who knows himself, knows the Lord."[15] The *Tao Te Ching*, which was written by Lao Tzu and has been translated more than any other book except than the Bible says:

> Knowing others is intelligence; knowing yourself is true wisdom. Mastering others is strength; mastering yourself is true power.[16]

And using somewhat different terminology, Jesus said:

> When you know yourselves, then you will be known, and will understand that you are children of the living Father. But if you do not know yourselves, then you live in poverty, and embody poverty.[17]

There is no better environment for learning about ourselves than the one in which we earn our living; it provides continual opportunities to observe what motivates us, frightens us, angers us and enlivens us. I have been fortunate to have been professionally involved in the business of managing other people's money for a period spanning four decades. While not all experiences have been pleasant or fruitful, they have been enormously helpful in clarifying a number of important issues about life's most fundamental questions. The securities markets represent the hopes and fears, loves and hates of a vast cross-section of humanity; they evoke the full gamut of psychological reactions. Through the pursuit of worldly goals—with money as a prime facilitator—we experience emotions that range from exhilaration to depression. In fact, everything we think or do swings us to and fro around a central tendency or core. In this sense, the securities markets are a metaphor for life as prices continually move from over-valued to under-valued and levels of optimism and pessimism rise and fall.

One of the best ways to achieve insightful breakthroughs is to follow a rigorous program of thorough self-observation. This simply means paying close attention to everything; being open-minded, curious and detached. In other words, making a commitment to observe and remember everything that occurs regardless of personal beliefs, preferences or fears. This is hard to do and takes a great deal of practice. Because the investment business provides instant feedback on the judgments that must be constantly made, advisors who analyze their emotions and personality quirks carefully and objectively have a much better chance of reducing future mistakes. While other professions also provide opportunities for mistakes, it is unlikely the feedback is as instantaneous or as frequent as it is in the goldfish-bowl environment of the investment business. To quote Edward C. Johnson II, one of the deans of Wall Street and the longtime head of the Fidelity Mutual Fund Complex:

> Because the conscious and subconscious human mind is so vast—the stock market, by the way, is just a bunch of minds—that there is no science, no IBM machine, no anything of that sort, that can tame it. What this means to us in practical affairs is that if we are able to do the thing that Americans find very hard to do—that is, *understand ourselves* (emphasis added) to some degree—we have a chance of becoming effective stock operators. That is a hard thing and a rare thing.[18]

Dealing with money forces one to come to grips with aspects of the self that are too often avoided. In the investment arena, this means scrutinizing financial and psychological limitations, both real and imagined. Do we prefer to eat well or sleep well? Not an easy decision; the emotions of greed and fear cloud most investors' perceptions and objectivity. Many times, clients have come to our office with the unequivocal desire to minimize risk. After a period of time, during which the investment climate has been unusually hospitable, they ask about the desirability of changing their objectives so their money is invested more aggressively. Assuming their circumstances have not changed, we discourage any deviation from their plan as it is not only counter to their original, more dispassionately determined desires but, more times than not, the wrong time to be taking increased risks. In fact, this has proven to be an excellent guide to an impending change in market direction; investors inevitably want to buy at market tops and sell when their securities have fared poorly, that is, at or near lows. It is amazing how reasonable people, who buy as many of their goods and services as possible on sale, want to buy securities at full price and shy away from purchasing them when they are at a discount to their intrinsic value. Those who know themselves don't have to know anything else to know everything else.

FOLLOWING THE HERD

Investors must also learn to guard against getting caught up in the herd instinct of the mass mind. People tend to follow the behavior of their peers whether choosing a doctor, restaurant or investment. If individuals learn that their contemporaries favor something, even when it is counter to their own opinion, they tend to stick with their peers, rationalizing that the majority must know what they are doing. This lemming-like behavior is understandable; it takes a great deal of self-confidence to stand up to a wave of opposing opinion. Taking a position that is contrary to the majority's is usually successful, not only in the field of investing, but in most of our day-to-day activities. In 1929, as an example, stocks had advanced for many years but the nearly universal opinion was that they would inevitably go higher. The 1929 financial panic illustrates the principle that when opinion becomes that one-sided, it is usually wrong. The same thing happened on a smaller scale in the 1980s as "everyone" was sure that real estate prices had nowhere to go but up. After all, "no one is making any more land" and prices had been going up for as long as most people cared to remember. Eventually the crowd was proven wrong and the experience that resulted from following the majority was, at a minimum, disappointing.

QUICK FIX OR COMPLETELY FIXED

Where are we now? How does the majority view our current state of affairs? As widely reported in the press, the problems of modern society—crime, pollution, education, poverty and job security—seem overwhelming if not insoluble. Political corruption and incompetence make the situation appear even more desperate. As immense as our problems seem, they are not new in either magnitude or character. Past periods of adversity have provided fertile ground for planting seeds of renewal; today is no different. Beneath the surface there is a growing awareness of our problems, and an increasing desire to get on with the task at hand. Once critical mass is achieved—the hundredth monkey effect—our insurmountable problems will be attacked and, in time, seem more like an exciting challenge than a daunting crisis.

As we enter the twenty-first century, signs of renewal are appearing throughout society, and business is beginning to lead the way. The restructuring, downsizing, and outsourcing strategies now prevalent force companies to rethink their objectives and become more selective with regard to the values and priorities they want to pursue. Sometimes this new spirit descends from boardroom initiatives and sometimes it emanates from employees at the grassroots level. I frequently speak to corporate executives and read hundreds of annual reports and other corporate communications; it has become clear to me that there is a transformation taking place. Excerpts from three different corporate reports are indicative of this new attitude:

> Diversity is much more than a program or legal requirement at HP; it is a business priority. . . . A culture that fosters respect for and appreciation of differences among people clearly helps teamwork, productivity and morale.
>
> . . . HEWLETT-PACKARD CORPORATION, *Annual Report*

We continue to demand of ourselves the strongest possible commitment to environmental excellence in all our operations worldwide. This steadfast commitment is an absolute necessity as we strive to meet society's expectations, achieve our business goals and live up to our long held values of environmental stewardship and good corporate citizenship.

> . . . POLAROID CORPORATION, *Report on the Environment*

Right now I feel like I imagine pro basketball players feel— they're doing exactly what they like to do, and getting paid for it. That's the way it is at Saturn: People depending on one another. People pulling in the same direction. It feels good.

> . . . KEVIN HAWKINS in *Powertrain Assembly—
> Saturn Homecoming Commemorative Magazine*

These comments are representative of the sentiments of a growing number of companies worldwide. Subsequent chapters will detail the ways businesses are incorporating humanistic values into their company's culture. While the trend is undeniably positive, many changes have been on an impromptu or fragmentary basis. Some companies have placed primary emphasis on quality-of-life issues that are of greatest concern to their employees, others have become much more concerned with community and environmental issues, still others have made enhanced opportunities for women and minorities a top priority. The solutions to these and most other business issues are unalterably connected. Yet many businesses have tried to resolve the concerns of their various constituencies by looking at them with a cursory, unconnected view. Rather than getting to the root cause of the problems and thinking in whole-system terms, they have tried to alleviate dissatisfactions by dealing with some aspect of a limited subsystem or by concentrating only on superficial effects.

Part of the difficulty in making these necessary changes is that the function of the rational mind is to break things down into separate parts so they can be more easily analyzed. The long term solution to most problems, however, necessitates looking at the interdependence of everything and discovering the common ground that unites seemingly distinct parts. Until problems are analyzed from a total system point of view, separative solutions are more likely to result in ineffective patchwork or temporary stopgaps. As businesses continue to re-examine their priorities and re-assesses their values, they will be well served if they formulate their policies around principles that are both holistically grounded and pragmatically sound. Ageless wisdom provides the all inclusive, practical framework around which a true and enduring guiding ethic can be built. More specifically, Hermetic Sciences, a nonsectarian, scientifically based description of reality, establishes the ideal model; one that is both comprehensive and efficacious. While some of the terminology and concepts may initially be unfamiliar, the ideas incorporated in the teachings will likely resonate at an intuitive level.

The next chapter describes the seven Hermetic Principles in some detail. The principles are repeated, along with practical illustrations, throughout the book. Showing how these universal laws relate to business enterprises worldwide is the objective of chapters three through nine.

NOTES

1. Vaclav Havel. Speech on the occasion of the Liberty Medal Ceremony, Philadelphia, 4 July 1994.

2. Dan Gottlieb. "On Healing," *Philadelphia Inquirer*, 19 June 1995, p. 5(G).

3. Anita Roddick. "Anita Roddick Speaks Out on Corporate Responsibility," *The Body Shop Lectures II* (West Sussex: The Body Shop International plc, 1994), pp. 2, 5.

4. Robert Bezi and George H. Gallup, Jr. "Seeking Spiritual Renewal," *Philadelphia Inquirer*, 25 December 1994, p. 7(D).

5. Ewart Rouse. "Book Chains Escalate War of Supremacy," *Philadelphia Inquirer*, 22 April 1996, p. 6(C).

6. Kenneth Miller. "Star Struck: A Journey to the New Frontiers of the Zodiac," *Life*, July 1997, p. 40.

7. Michele Galen and Karen West. "Companies Hit the Road Less Traveled," *Business Week*, 5 June 1995, pp. 82–85. Reprinted from the June 5, 1995 issue of *Business Week* by permission. © 1995 by McGraw-Hill Companies.

8. Lawrence Minard. "The Principle of Maximum Pessimism," *Forbes*, 16 January 1995, p. 71.

9. Krishna Kripalani, ed. *All Men Are Brothers: Autobiographical Reflections* (New York: Continuum, 1994), p. 69.

10. Huston Smith. *Forgotten Truth: The Common Vision of the World's Religions* (New York: HarperCollins, 1992), front cover.

11. Aldous Huxley. *The Perennial Philosophy* (New York: Harper & Row, 1945), p. vii.

12. John White. *What Is Enlightenment?* (Los Angeles: Jeremy P. Tarcher, 1985), p. xv.

13. Antoine Faivre. *The Eternal Hermes: From Greek God to Alchemical Magus*, trans. Joscelyn Godwin (Grand Rapids, MI: Phanes Press, 1995), p. 104.

14. Ken Wilber. *Up From Eden: A Transpersonal View of Human Evolution* (Boulder, CO: Shambhala Publications, 1983), p. 7.

15. Philip Novak. *The World's Wisdom: Sacred Texts of the World's Religions* (San Francisco: HarperCollins, 1994), p. 323.

16. Ibid., p. 163.

17. *The Secret Teachings of Jesus: Four Gnostic Gospels*, trans. (with intro. & notes) Marvin W. Meyer (New York: Random House, 1984), p. 19.

18. Edward C. Johnson, II. "Contrary Opinion in Stock Market Techniques," in *Classics: An Investor's Anthology*, ed. Charles D. Ellis with James R. Vertin (Homewood, IL: Business One Irwin, 1989), p. 397.

2

Old Wisdom—
New Understanding

The twentieth century has seen the scientific community's worldview come ever closer to what mystics have described for thousands of years. Discoveries first made by Einstein and later corroborated and built upon by other physicists, dramatically altered the previously accepted Newtonian worldview. Newton's concepts of absolute space and time, elementary solid particles and the idea of an objective description of nature were shattered by atomic physics and relativity theory. According to the latter, space is not three-dimensional and time cannot be separated from the rest of reality. The two are intimately connected and form a four-dimensional continuum of "space-time."[1] Physicist David Bohm, a protégé of Einstein's, expressed this idea as follows:

> One is led to a new notion of unbroken wholeness which denies the classical idea of analyzability of the world into separate and independently existing parts. . . . Rather, we say that inseparable quantum interconnectedness of the whole universe is the fundamental reality, and that relatively independently behaving parts are merely particular and contingent forms within this whole.[2]

The idea that there is a distinction between time and space has been so ingrained in our description of natural phenomena that a modification of this thought requires a radical adjustment to our understanding of physical objects. Based on this new comprehension, solids, liquids and gases are nothing but forms of energy.[3] If an object is equivalent to a certain amount of energy, its mass can no longer be viewed as static. Mass must, therefore, be depicted as a dynamic process or pattern. Under these circumstances, the traditional concepts of space and time and of independent particles lose much of their meaning.[4] These relativistic descriptions of modern physics are illusory because we do not experience the four-dimensional space-time world with our senses, but observe only its three-dimensional "images." The three-dimensional reality we witness daily is merely a projection of higher realms just as two-dimensional shadows are reflections of three-dimensional objects that encompass our reality. The relativistic model closely parallels two fundamental elements of most mystical cosmologies—the basic oneness of the universe and its inherently dynamic character.[5] This description of the unity of life is contained in the tenth discourse of the Bhagavad-Gita, the great epic poem of the Mahabharata:

> I am the Self, . . . dwelling in the heart of all beings, and the beginning, the middle, as well as the end of all beings. . . . Whatever is the seed of all beings, I am that. . . . There is no moving or unmoving entity that may exist without Me.[6]

While the views of modern science and ageless wisdom have been converging, there remain significant differences. Science relies upon sensory observations in controlled settings for its information about the universe. Mystics, on the other hand, teach that the fundamental questions of life can never be adequately described in words nor answered by sensory data.[7] The physical senses are not only limited but often deceiving. First, our sense of sight is often inadequate or at least subject to varying interpretations. Two people looking at the same optical illusion often report seeing two distinctly different objects. Our sense of sight leads us to believe that the earth is flat and the sun moves around an apparently stationary earth. Light from the sun takes eight minutes to reach us; in that time the sun could have exploded even though we think we are looking at an object still in existence. Second, it is well known that human senses perceive only a minute percentage of the total light and sound spectrum. Thus the amount of sensory data that reaches our awareness is but a fraction of the total available. It certainly seems foolhardy to make definitive judgments about reality based largely on the limited physical evidence to which most humans have access. Temperature, taste, the loudness of a sound and the speed at which an object appears to move are all subject to significant distortion.[8] Albert Einstein put the futility of relying on our senses into perspective when he said:

> Up to the Twentieth Century, reality was everything humans could touch, smell, see, and hear. Since the initial publication of the chart of the electromagnetic spectrum, humans have learned that what they can touch, smell, see, and hear is less than one-millionth of reality.[9]

If data from the senses are unreliable and an observer is an integral though subjective part of every experiment, where can people turn to understand the world and their place in it? Ageless wisdom, basing its knowledge on intuitive insights, bypasses the senses and pulls directly from the fourth dimension of "space-time." Because intuition bypasses the physical, it cannot be explained in terms of the five senses. As a voice of the non-physical world, intuition can be thought of as a communication link between the personality and the soul.[10] Intuition and reason are not opposites, but complements. In order to access the levels where intuitive knowledge resides, it is necessary to apply all the rational analysis at our disposal; focusing our attention on a particular problem, searching our memories for clues about the subject under scrutiny and using our imagination to elicit the answers we seek. After this process has been pursued and the mind, in an act of capitulation, becomes silent, a flash of intuitive insight strikes in the form of a feeling, thought or image. Intuition leads us to the universal principles or laws that underlie our sense-based observations; knowledge that can be directly applied to the practical problem with which we began.

According to Marcia Emery, Ph.D., intuitive insights may be received before all the facts are available. Dr. Emery concludes an article on intuition with the following statement:

> The value of intuition is becoming more and more apparent, gaining respect as the silent but vital partner in any decision-making process. This well kept secret of successful business people across America is available to each and every one of us. It is not surprising that intuition is becoming the most important strategic business tool of the twenty-first century.[11]

Richard DeVos, the cofounder of Amway Corporation, believes that total dependence on facts limits the adventurous spirit so critical to the process of discovery and innovation. DeVos agrees with many leaders who believe that companies need to integrate intuition with facts and logic if they are to optimize the decision-making process.[12]

While a metaphysically based system that relies in large measure on intuitive knowledge may still be scoffed at by strict rationalists, age old descriptions of reality have proven to be astonishingly accurate. Long ago mystics described the creation of the universe in much the same terms as scientists currently use for what has come to be known as the "Big Bang Theory." Ancient astrologers, with uncanny accuracy, left places in their cosmology for the discovery of planets then unknown. Concepts such as the interconnectedness of all things and the experimenter's unavoidable participation in all observations, which have been acknowledged by physicists only recently, have been central tenets of ageless wisdom for thousands of years. As stated by the renowned scientist Robert Julius Oppenheimer:

. . . the general notions about human understanding and community which are illustrated by discoveries in atomic physics are not in the nature of things wholly unfamiliar, wholly unheard of, or new. Even in our own culture they have a history, and in Buddhist and Hindu thought a more considerable and central place. What we shall find is an exemplification, an encouragement, and a refinement of old wisdom.[13]

PRINCIPLES OF AGELESS WISDOM

It has been said that all of the esoteric wisdom of most spiritual traditions can be traced to Hermes' teachings. In fact, a student of comparative religions will quickly see the influence of the Hermetic Sciences on most religions. The thrust of Hermes' work, however, was in planting seeds rather than establishing a school of philosophy or theology. To this day we use the term "hermetic" to mean secret or sealed, in keeping with the practice of secrecy his followers observed in the imparting of these teachings.[14] The principles and axioms of Hermetic Sciences, accompanied by explanations and illustrations, are presented below. In the chapters that follow, we examine how these scientifically based principles are being applied to the world of business to improve our lives in the work place and beyond.

The Principle of Mentalism

"The All [God] is mind; the universe is mental."[15] Most of us are familiar with the phrases, "I think, therefore, I am," "we create our own reality," "mind over matter," "you are what you think," "the power of positive thought." We usually dismiss them as too trite or farfetched to be relevant to our daily lives, wondering how these sayings can possibly help us achieve our objectives or solve our problems. For thousands of years revered spiritual leaders have told us that only one thing exists (spirit, the animating force) and it is mental in nature. While appearing to split into two distinct forces (consciousness and matter), the only difference between them is the rate at which they vibrate; consciousness being

faster and subtler and matter being slower and grosser. Scientists have increasingly confirmed this unified description of reality. As Erwin Schrodinger, the well-known quantum physicist, stated: "Mind by its very nature is a *singulare tantum.* I should say: the overall number of minds is just one."[16]

Stanford University neurophysiologist Karl Pribram, one of the architects of our current understanding of the brain, has come to the conclusion that the universe may be a giant hologram, a kind of image or construct created by the human mind. To quote Dr. Pribram:

> It isn't that the world of appearances is wrong; it isn't that there aren't objects out there, at one level of reality. It's that if you penetrate through and look at the universe with a . . . holographic system, you arrive at a different view, a different reality. And that other reality can explain things that have hitherto remained inexplicable scientifically: paranormal phenomena, synchronicities, the apparently meaningful coincidences of events.[17]

The idea that only one thing exists has *mind*-shattering implications. Thoughts, the creations of the mind, are as real and potent as physical objects. Each of us can be a force for good or evil without ever getting out of bed. The skeptic will no doubt ask for proof of this assertion. Unfortunately, the vibrations of consciousness are so subtle that they cannot be detected by any material instrument. Only consciousness is able to comprehend consciousness.[18] Nonetheless, we are often physically aware of the vibrations of consciousness when others gesture or glare or use other forms of nonverbal communication.

There is also strong circumstantial evidence that thoughts can have an overriding influence on our health and well-being. Athletes have long made use of mental visualizations to improve their physical performance. The act of imagining running the perfect race or completing a flawless floor exercise can have a positive effect on the actual event. Dan Millman, a world-class trampoline champion and former gymnastics coach at a number of well-known universities, is quite familiar with the power of the mind. According to him, a gymnast will fall off a balance beam if the athlete's mind fails to remain squarely focused over the beam. In the same vein, two basketball players of equal size and skill can have vastly different results when attempting to make a basket based solely on their respective powers of concentration. Single-minded attention, which eliminates all mental distractions, is a potent ally.[19]

There have been many studies documenting the significant role played by the mind in the healing process. Based upon his experiences, Andrew Weil, author and Harvard-trained physician, is convinced that no bodily problem is beyond the reach of mental intervention.[20] Thoughts expressed as fear, guilt, anxiety, depression and resentment have very real physical consequences. Internationally known author Louise L. Hay has told how she was able to overcome cancer when she recognized that the source of her disease could be directly related to a childhood of oppressive abuse. The resentment was literally eating away at her body. With the help of a therapist she released the old anger and, forgoing the recommended medical and surgical treatment, underwent a thorough mental and physical cleansing. Six months after her diagnosis, doctors determined that she no longer had a trace of cancer.[21]

In his book, *Healing Words*, Larry Dossey, M.D., discusses the effectiveness of a different mental activity: prayer. As a prelude to his investigation of prayer, he examines the validity of long-distance intuitive diagnosis and remote sensing (mentally conveying complex information to widely separated individuals) and cites research which demonstrates that neither space nor time can confine the mind.[22] The efficacy of prayer is perhaps best illustrated in a study by cardiologist Randolph Byrd. Over a ten-month period, 393 patients admitted to the coronary care unit at San Francisco General Hospital were assigned by computer to one of two groups; 192 were prayed for by home prayer groups and the remaining 201 were not remembered in prayer. The study was rigidly designed as a randomized, double-blind experiment where neither the patients, nurses nor doctors knew which group the patients were in. The prayed-for group was five times less likely than the unremembered group to require antibiotics and three times less likely to develop pulmonary edema. None of the prayed-for group needed endotracheal intubation versus twelve in the unremembered group and fewer patients in the prayed-for group died. While some critics believe the study had flaws, Dr. Dossey suggests that if the technique being studied had been a new surgical procedure or experimental drug rather than prayer, the research would have been proclaimed a breakthrough.[23]

The futility of debating what influence the mental has on the physical is illustrated by the following story. A paranoid person believed she was dead. Despite extraordinary efforts, a psychiatrist was unable to change her patient's mind. In desperation the doctor asked if the patient believed that the dead feel pain. There was absolute agreement that they do not. Thereupon, the psychiatrist grabbed the patient and put her in an unrelenting hammer lock. The patient cried out in excruciating pain. "Aha," exclaimed the doctor, "you are alive!" "Wrong!" shouted the patient. "The dead do feel pain!"[24] What we "know" is surely a function of what we believe.

The Principle of Vibration

"Nothing rests; Everything moves; Everything vibrates."[25] The Principle of Vibration tells us that everything, from mind to matter, is in constant motion. If electrons ever stop orbiting the nuclei of atoms, the world as we know it would cease to exist. Sound and light are part of the electromagnetic activity of the universe. Sound is an atmospheric vibration that we can hear; color is reflected light vibrations that we visually perceive. While all vibrations are qualitatively equal, oscillations from 16 to 20,000 cycles per second are generally audible to the human ear; those on either side of this range generally inaudible. Our

perception of light is likewise confined to a specific range of vibration.[26]

The differences among various phenomena are simply functions of the rapidity of pulsation. Lowering the vibratory activity of water reduces its temperature and eventually turns the water into ice crystals. Raising the temperature by increasing the vibratory rate changes the ice back to water and, if the vibratory activity is accelerated further, the water becomes steam and then disappears from our sensory perception. The application of vibrations to raise the temperature of food is the principle behind the operation of a microwave oven.

To see the interconnection between sound and light and, by extension, everything else, consider a spinning top or wheel. When the top begins moving it can be seen easily with little if any sound being heard. By increasing the speed, a low-pitched sound may be discerned. As the speed is increased further, the sound or note rises progressively in the musical scale. Finally, a shrill, piercing sound is followed by silence as the rate of motion becomes so high that it is beyond the range of the human ear. Next comes the perception of rising degrees of heat. After some time, the eye begins to see a dark reddish color. As the speed is increased, the red brightens and turns successively into orange, yellow, green, blue, indigo and violet. At even faster speeds, the color disappears as the vibrations move past the range of the human eye. Nonetheless, invisible emanations of "x-rays" continue as the object's constitution changes. Electricity and magnetism are next emitted. Eventually, the vibratory rate reaches a point where the molecules disintegrate and return to the original atoms which become finer and finer substances eventually returning to the primal source.[27]

All motion involves change, transformation, modification and variation. As a flower sprouts, blossoms, withers, dies and then begins the process all over again, the principle of vibration assures us that life is an infinite series of births and deaths and that impermanence is a necessary and beneficial aspect of creation.

The Principle of Correspondence

"As above, so below; As below, so above."[28] There is an exact correlation and agreement among all levels of existence from the lowest to the highest. This principle holds for the animal, vegetable or mineral kingdom and for levels transcending those with which we are familiar. Therefore, if we discover certain fixed laws in one area we may, by analogy, conclude that the same quality exists in other areas. This follows from the previous axiom which states that the only difference among parts of the universe is the rate of their vibration. We should, therefore, be able to relate any part of God's expression to those within our own range of experience.[29] Just as the principles of geometry allow us, while remaining here on Earth, to measure stars and their projected movements, so the principle of correspondence enables us to reason intelligently from the known to the unknown.[30] Andrew Weil expresses this in biological terms:

> This [As above, so below; as below, so above.] means that patterns of truth observed at any level of reality will be true at every level of reality. Therefore, if we can discern the operation of the healing system at any level of biological organization, we should be able to infer the nature of its operation at other levels.[31]

Those scientifically inclined can look at the construction of an atom to see this principle at work. Within each atom in our body, or in the universe for that matter, varying numbers of electrons circle around a nucleus. The nucleus, where the atomic mass is concentrated, is only a thousand-billionth of a centimeter in size. The electrons extend out to a distance of about a hundred-millionth of a centimeter. By far the greater part of the atom is empty space.[32] The electrons move around the center in much the same way the planets orbit the sun. In relative terms, the distance between the electrons and the nucleus corresponds to the distance between the planets and the sun.

Another illustration of this principle is evident when we observe how we organize to accomplish our everyday activities and compare it to prophetic descriptions of the hierarchical structure of the universe. The scriptures tell us that God begins a cycle of manifestation by thinking it into existence. The created, having been made in the image of the Creator and given free will, continue the process of creation. In much the same way a founder or creator of an enterprise usually provides the broad vision and then calls upon executives and assistants to carry out the details. Furthermore, every creative act involves four steps. First comes the idea. Then a plan or blueprint is drawn. Next a mold or process is developed. Finally, the product or result is brought to fruition. This fourfold process is followed on all levels from the highest to the lowest.

The Principle of Polarity

"Everything is dual; everything has poles; everything has its pairs of opposites; like and unlike are the same; opposites are identical in nature, but different in degree; extremes meet; all truths are but half-truths; all paradoxes may be reconciled."[33] The Principle of Polarity proclaims that everything has two sides or aspects with innumerable gradations between the extremes. The one and the many are but two poles of the same thing differentiated only by their respective vibration rates. The same is true of heat and cold, light and dark, noise and quiet, good and bad, courage and fear, ad infinitum. The status of each pair is relative and each can be changed into the other; hot becomes cold, light turns to dark, wet becomes dry, etc. In fact, it is impossible to determine objectively where heat ends and cold begins. There is no absolute heat or absolute cold; each simply indicates varying degrees, or vibrations, of the same thing. The same can be said for love and hate. At their mid-point, like and dislike blend into each other and it becomes increasingly difficult to differentiate between the two.[34]

In order for consciousness to evolve, the unity that underlies reality must appear to be separated into a world of duality. Otherwise, movement would be limited and none of the resistance required to build form would exist. This illusory separation enables self-conscious awareness to expand as one is forced to make choices and, thereby, learns to discriminate among the variety of physical objects and mental conditions that constitute life.

The wave-particle duality of quantum physics, in which the same electron can take the form of either a wave or a particle, forced scientists to come to terms with the polarity paradox. Initially, it seems illogical that light can be both a wave and a particle. A wave is like a continuous abstract form of motion; a particle more like a point or bullet. Although it is difficult to comprehend how both terms can describe the same thing, experiments have conclusively proven that light can take the form of either waves or particles.[35] Danish physicist Niels Bohr introduced the concept of complementarity as a way to reconcile this wave-particle question. The concept of complementarity leads to the understanding that because one view is right, the opposite is not necessarily wrong. Viewing a coin from the head's side provides one point of view; the tail's side gives us an entirely different perspective. Nonetheless, they are both part of the same indivisible coin.

Eastern philosophers have long held that all apparent opposites are, in fact, two sides of the same coin. To them, pairs of opposites constitute a complementary relationship, where each of the two poles is dynamically linked to the other. While acknowledging the individuality of things, these philosophers are acutely aware that all differences and contrasts are only relative within an all-encompassing unity. Life's highest goal is to attain a state of being wherein all opposites are recognized as polar and, therefore, form a unity. In the words of D.T. Suzuki:

> The fundamental idea of Buddhism is to pass beyond the world of opposites, a world built up by intellectual distinction and

emotional defilement, and to realize the spiritual world of nondistinction, which involves achieving an absolute point of view.[36]

Taoists, likewise, view the world as a ceaseless interaction of the complementary forces of yin and yang. Failure to comprehend the unity of opposites leads to many problems as recounted below in the first verse and reconciled in the partially reproduced second verse from the *Tao Te Ching:*

> When people see some things as beautiful, other things become ugly. When people see some things as good, other things become bad.
> Being and non-being create each other. Difficult and easy support each other. Long and short define each other. High and low depend on each other. Before and after follow each other. . . .[37]

Realizing that all coins have two sides and that all truths are but half truths encourages us to be open to all points of view.

The Principle of Rhythm

"Everything flows out and in; everything has its tides; all things rise and fall; the pendulum-swing manifests in everything; the measure of the swing to the right is the measure of the swing to the left; rhythm compensates."[38] Rhythm is measured motion between the two poles described by the Principle of Polarity, demonstrating the close link between these two principles. While rarely reaching the extreme of either pole, movement is always toward one pole and then back toward the other. From emotional states which oscillate between euphoria and depression to geopolitical movements involving the rise and fall of nations, everything follows rhythmic patterns. There are ceaseless actions and reactions; advances and retreats; risings and sinkings embodied in all phenomena. The swing in one direction determines the extent of the movement in the other; rhythm compensates.

There may be long periods of time between counterbalancing actions and, as a result, we are often unaware of how events from a remote past are causing our current experiences. From the recognition of this principle, it logically follows that no action circumvents the law of compensation and that undeviating justice prevails throughout the universe.[39]

Modern physicists picture matter as continuously moving in rhythmic patterns that are determined by molecular, atomic and nuclear structures. An alternating dance of expansion and contraction is forever spiraling forth. All particles interact by emitting and reabsorbing energy. Subatomic particles not only perform an energy dance, they are an energy dance; a pulsating process of creation and destruction.[40] As an example, consider spiraling clouds of hydrogen gas that form to create stars. First the gas expands into a ball of fire. After millions of years, when most of the hydrogen fuel has been consumed, the star begins to contract. Contraction continues until the star collapses. From this condition, the star awaits another impulse which will ignite yet another solar life cycle.[41]

The Principle of Cause and Effect

"Every Cause has its Effect; every Effect has its Cause; everything happens according to Law; Chance is but a name for Law not recognized; there are many planes of causation, but nothing escapes the Law."[42] The Principle of Cause and Effect states that nothing happens by chance; what appears to be chance is simply an unrecognized cause. Law and order prevail throughout the universe. There is a relationship among everything that has gone before and everything that follows. For example, a person has two parents, four grandparents, eight great-grandparents and so on until, after forty generations, this person has millions of ancestors. In the same way, the number of causes behind even the smallest of events grows geometrically. Thus, all our thoughts and all our actions have both a direct and indirect impact on the course of causation.[43]

Isaac Newton's third law of motion, that for every action there is an equal and opposite reaction, is a scientific restatement of the principle of cause and effect. A jet airplane engine may be the most well known practical application of Newton's third law.[44] The plane is thrust forward (the effect) as a result of gases blasting rearward (the cause). With regard to Newton, it is interesting to note that when John Maynard Keynes bought and inspected a trunk full of his papers, he was shocked to find that Newton spent as much time studying alchemy and numerology as he did calculating his laws of motion.[45]

What is cause and what is effect is not always easy to determine. In fact, it is frequently difficult to trace anything back to its initial cause. What causes crime: drugs, poverty, lack of jobs, poor educational system, not enough prisons, too many prisons? What causes disease: poor nutrition, heredity, stress, cold weather, wet weather? It is often impossible to unravel the effect from the complex of circumstances that surround it; for example, a drug that is used to remedy one health problem often causes others. Our dualistic state of mind, wherein we think in either/or terms, clouds our ability to see the whole picture.

The Principle of Gender

"Gender is in everything; everything has its Masculine and Feminine Principles; Gender manifests on all planes."[46] The Principle of Gender declares that the masculine and feminine elements or principles are present and continually active in all phases of life. This principle can generate confusion because people often assume that it refers to the physical differences between men and women. The term refers to the whole creative process and is, therefore, used in a much larger context. Differences between the sexes are only one small aspect of the Principle of Gender.

Putting this principle in a scientific context, consider again the composition of an atom. An atom consists of a number of negatively charged electrons circling around a positively charged nucleus. The positive particles exert an influence upon the negative particles which eventually results in "creating" or "generating" an atom. The masculine element correlates with the positive pole and the feminine with the negative. No inferiority or superiority is implied by the use of these terms; the two are equal but perform different functions. When an electron (feminine, negative charge) leaves or becomes detached from an atom it actively seeks a masculine or positively charged particle. When the union takes place the feminine particles vibrate rapidly and circle the masculine particles thereby producing a new atom. The feminine is the one doing the active creative work at the instigation or stimulation of the masculine. In some forms of life, both elements are combined in one organism. In fact, everything contains some of each of the two elements. The phenomena of attraction, repulsion, chemical affinity, cohesion, and gravitation are all manifestations of the gender principle.[47]

The Principle of Gender extends to mental as well as physical realms. The masculine element of mind corresponds to the self-conscious, objective aspects, while the feminine element corresponds to the subconscious, subjective phases. The feminine element receives impressions and generates new thoughts and ideas. Creative imagination is under her domain. The masculine element tends to work in the direction of expressing or projecting. It is stimulative and primarily concerned with the work of the will in its many aspects.[48] This includes organizing, analyzing and discriminating. Successful actors, orators, politicians, preachers and writers, both male and female, make use of the masculine element. When balanced with the nurturing, synthesizing and generating facilities of the female principle, the full spectrum of human accomplishment becomes possible.[49]

Phil Jackson, former professional basketball player and coach, discusses the gender principle in his book, *Sacred Hoops*. He relates that he was a much more effective coach when he was able to balance the masculine and feminine sides of his nature. He attributes his success in integrating these two qualities to his wife who showed him how to temper his aggressive, masculine instincts with his compassionate, feminine side.

In my case, healing the split between feminine and masculine, heart and mind—as symbolized by my compassionate father and analytic mother—has been an essential aspect of my growth both as a coach and a human being.[50]

A brief summary of the seven Hermetic Principles is now in order. Everything in existence is a *mental* creation. God literally thinks the universe into existence, beginning with the idea of what It wants to create. Once begun, a spiral or whirling motion is produced which causes everything to *vibrate*. The only difference between spirit and matter is the rate at which they vibrate. Because everything is made of the same essence, the same principles apply to all gradations of being. Thus a *correspondence* exists among all levels of creation, enabling self-conscious organisms to comprehend and empathize with each other. Self-consciousness requires the appearance of *duality* although all opposites are identical in nature but different in degree. Opposites swing back and forth in *rhythmic* motion always seeking a state of balance or equilibrium. This to-and-fro movement *causes effects* that reverberate throughout the cosmos. The life cycle continues to generate more evolved organisms as the projective *masculine principle* stimulates the receptive *feminine principle* and the latter takes the seed idea of the former and produces new forms.

The practical applications and ramifications of these principles, as they relate to the world of business, are discussed in the ensuing chapters.

NOTES

1. Fritjof Capra. *The Tao of Physics* (New York: Bantam Books, 1975), p. 50.

2. D. Bohm and B. Hiley. "On the Intuitive Understanding of Nonlocality as Implied by Quantum Theory," *Foundations of Physics* 5 (1975), pp. 96, 102.

3. Capra, p. 51.

4. Ibid, p. 67.

5. Ibid, pp. 158–59.

6. Swami Rama. *Perennial Psychology of the Bhagavad Gita* (Honesdale, PA: Himalayan International Institute, 1985), p. 323.

7. Capra, p. 16.

8. Morris Kline. *Mathematics and the Search for Knowledge* (New York: Oxford University Press, 1985), pp. 30–31.

9. Thomas Claire. *Bodywork: What Type of Massage to Get—and How to Make the Most of It* (New York: William Morrow & Co., 1995), p. 247.

10. Gary Zukav. *The Seat of the Soul*, A Fireside Book (New York: Simon & Schuster, 1989), p. 199.

11. Marcia Emery. "Intuition: the Spark that Ignites Vision," *The New Leaders*, January/February 1995, p. 2.

12. Ibid.

13. Robert J. Oppenheimer. *Science and the Common Understanding* (New York: Oxford University Press, 1954), pp. 9–10.

14. Three Initiates. *The Kybalion* (Chicago: The Yogi Publication Society, 1912), pp. 17–22.

15. Ibid, p. 26.

16. Larry Dossey, M.D. *Healing Words: The Power of Prayer and the Practice of Medicine* (San Francisco: HarperSanFrancisco, 1993), p. 43.

17. Daniel Goleman. "Holographic Memory: Karl Pribram Interviewed by Daniel Goleman," *Psychology Today*, February 1979, pp. 83–84.

18. Paramahansa Yogananda. *Scientific Healing Affirmations* (Los Angeles: Self-Realization Fellowship, 1981), p. 29.

19. Dan Millman. *The Warrior Athlete: Body, Mind & Spirit* (Walpole, NH: Stillpoint Publishing, 1979), p. 58.

20. Andrew Weil, M.D. *Spontaneous Healing* (New York: Alfred A. Knopf, 1995), p. 97.

21. Louise L. Hay. *You Can Heal Your Life* (Santa Monica, CA: Hay House, 1984), p. 201.

22. Dossey, pp. 49–50.

23. Ibid, p. 180.

24. Ibid, p. 204.

25. Three Initiates, p. 137.

26. Yogananda, p. 28.

27. Three Initiates, p. 144.

28. Ibid, p. 113.

29. *The One and the Many* (Chicago: A.C. McClurg & Company, 1909), p. 62.

30. Three Initiates, p. 29.

31. Weil, p. 71.

32. Paul Davies. *God and the New Physics* (New York: Simon & Schuster, 1983), p. 146.

33. Three Initiates, p. 149.

34. Ibid, p. 34.

35. K. C. Cole. *Sympathetic Vibrations: Reflections on Physics as a Way of Life*, with a Foreword by Frank Oppenheimer (New York: Bantam Books, 1985), p. 210.

36. Capra, pp. 130–131.

37. Novak, p. 161.

38. Three Initiates, p. 159.

39. Ibid, p. 160.

40. Capra, p. 232.

41. Ibid, p. 180.

42. Three Initiates, p. 171.

43. Ibid, pp. 171–177.

44. *Compton's Interactive Encyclopedia* 1996 ed., s.v. "Reaction Engines" [CD-ROM] (Compton's NewMedia, 1995).

45. Jacob Bronowski. "Black Magic and White Magic," in *The World Treasury of Physics, Astronomy, and Mathematics*, ed. Timothy Ferris, with a Foreword by Clifton Fadiman, genl. ed. (Boston: Little, Brown & Co., 1991), p. 810.

46. Three Initiates, p. 183.

47. Ibid, pp. 183–191.

48. Ibid, pp. 194–203.

49. Ibid, p. 207.

50. Phil Jackson and Hugh Delehanty. *Sacred Hoops: Spiritual Lessons of a Hardwood Warrior*, with a Foreword by Senator Bill Bradley (New York: Hyperion, 1995), p. 67.

3

The Origin of Competition

Ageless wisdom tells us that life is a school for souls in which the "students" discover, and then learn to live in harmony with, the laws and principles discussed in chapter two. In the evolutionary journey back to THE CREATOR our consciousness expands as we travel the learning curve of life. Humanity is now at a point where its sense of separated individuality is beginning to open, both scientifically and spiritually, to an awareness of the interconnectedness of all things.

Not all souls are at the same level of development. While most souls may, figuratively speaking, be in high school, some are early in the educational process, others are close to graduation. Ageless wisdom has numerous terms for the grades or stages that everyone follows. We have used the following business related categorizations which are closely aligned with the five stages of ancient wisdom: Competition, Cooperation, Cocreation, Responsibility and Inclusion. People will behave in accordance with their stage of development. There is no one standard of conduct and no particular stage is better than any other. A high school student is no better than someone in elementary school and a child in kindergarten is not expected to have the same self-control and consideration for others as would be expected from a person close to graduation. Moreover, it is practically impossible for students to determine with any precision the status of their fellow pupils.[1] Further complicating the process is the fact that some facets of our consciousness may be quite advanced while others are making progress more slowly. Examples of this paradox are frequently in the news. A number of our most venerated religious and spiritual leaders have been forced to resign in disgrace because of revelations of disreputable activities in their secular lives. Political and business luminaries, many of whom have been renowned for their philanthropy, have been removed from high office, even incarcerated, due to conduct that was morally or legally reprehensible. Everyone's personality, even those who have achieved material success or reverence as a spiritual leader, has elements that need further attention. Only the soul that is very advanced is free from the wheel of birth, death and rebirth. No matter what our current status, we have spent some time in every grade on our way to graduation. It should be helpful, therefore, to trace our progress from early in the evolutionary process when feelings of isolation and separation were the norm. Understanding this history will enable us to recognize who we are, where we are going, and how best to reach our destination.

Eons ago, humans needed an effective fight or flight mechanism to protect them from the ravages of the jungle. If a wild animal was about to attack there was no time to contemplate a response. Our ancestors were programmed to react automatically to "others" as potential threats and thus were dominated by fear, paranoia and self-centeredness. As the transition from unconscious, instinctive behavior to self-conscious, reasoned behavior began, a survival mentality forced them to be ever alert and outwardly observant.[2] In these early stages of development, humans naturally made many mistakes. Those that will be discussed in the sections that follow are: first, a misplaced identification with the body; second, the assumption that happiness is a function of accumulating more material things or engaging in more pleasurable experiences; third, the conviction that the world's resources are unduly limited; and fourth, the belief that all creatures are separate and autonomous.

BODY AND SOUL

A mistaken identification with the physical body leads to a condition in which people rely exclusively on sensory data and, therefore, base decisions on superficial appearances. The underlying assumptions at this stage are what the late Willis Harman, former President of the Institute of Noetic Sciences and emeritus professor at Stanford University, has labeled the M-1 Metaphysic. The basic stuff of the universe is matter. Consciousness apart from a living physical organism is not only unknown, it is inconceivable.[3] Under this worldview, we consider the organs of our body as independent parts and treat them as if they operated in a vacuum. We separate our body from our emotions and try to get rid of the symptom rather than the cause of the problem. We are not responsible for our "disease" for it is caused by something external to us.[4] It is not surprising, therefore, that we think of ourselves as our bodies rather than our souls. This inaccurate identification of the "I" is a necessary part of the evolutionary process; it generates mistakes which force us into new ways of thinking and acting. Our awareness expands as we endeavor, through trial and error, to find solutions to our body-centered problems. The pain inflicted by our mistakes sharpens our reasoning and discriminatory powers. We begin to analyze experiences and cultivate independent thought, thereby rejecting the cultural prejudices that inhibit our progress.[5] The more closely we examine our beliefs and desires the greater our progress in aligning with universal laws and identifying with our true essence.

PAIN AND PLEASURE

As we become more mindful, we need different, less restricting experiences to continue our growth. At this point we no longer need the same level of instinctual behavior that was necessary in the jungle. With day-to-day survival less of a concern, our focus shifts to the attainment of pleasure and the avoidance of pain. It is generally believed that the more pleasure we have in the form of money, power, sex, prestige, etc., the closer we will be to true happiness. We eventually find, however, that fulfilling our sensual and emotional desires does not bring the happiness we had expected. We may feel happy momentarily but this is often followed by a fear of losing what we just acquired. Or it may be followed by the realization that our acquisition is not as exciting as anticipated; it is anticlimactic and a letdown ensues. For example, when we acquire a new car, we are filled with excitement. A few months later our enthusiasm wanes and our attention shifts to the high cost of auto insurance or the fear that someone will spill food on the new upholstery. A related belief is that if getting something made us happy, more of it would make us even happier. But the law of diminishing returns soon sets in. This law states that as more units of the same product are consumed the value or appreciation of the item diminishes relative to the preceding units.[6] The second scoop of ice cream is less enjoyable than the first and the third less than the second. Pleasurable experiences and material possessions add spice to life but they do not enable us to achieve our highest aspirations.

PAIN AND PLEASURE WALL STREET STYLE

The investment profession provides ample opportunities for making mistakes; I have learned more from a few embarrassingly poor investments than from all those that were successful. One of my most regretted decisions involved a company whose stock price gyrated widely, with my emotions following close behind.

The holy grail of the investment business is the "next" Microsoft, Intel or Coca-Cola. In the 1980s I thought I had found it. JWP was a unique international service company engaged primarily in designing, installing and maintaining high-tech equipment built by others. The company's sales, assets and earnings grew very rapidly during the eighties and by the early nineties revenues exceeded $4 billion. A number of our clients saw their investment in the company's stock increase tenfold. Then, for no apparent reason, the stock started a precipitous decline. Most Wall Street analysts following the company continued to recommend the stock. Based on publicly available information, the company's fundamentals warranted a much higher stock price; I could not find any justification for selling the stock.

Over a period of many months, pieces of a deteriorating financial picture began to emerge. It felt like Chinese water torture. Then two of the company's well-known and internationally respected vendors issued letters expressing confidence in and support for the company.[7] This was followed by a well regarded executive, David Sokol, being brought in as president to turn the business around; I felt relieved. Within months of taking the helm, Sokol quit citing some accounting irregularities at the company. With one of the largest accounting firms in the world monitoring the books, this accusation seemed hard to believe. The board of directors indicated Mr. Sokol's abrupt departure was simply a ploy to wrest control from current management; I was confused. Part of me rationalized that this was a only temporary setback as JWP was the dominant company in an industry that had grown rapidly and had an exceedingly bright future. Despite what I thought was a very rational evaluation of the situation, something bothered me. I could not put my finger on the source of my uneasiness, but I was not comfortable. Numerous nights were spent awake restlessly looking at every possibility. It was not long before my worst fears were realized; the company declared bankruptcy and, sometime later, admitted to engaging in fraudulent accounting practices.[8] Because some profits had been realized when the stock was flying high and the cost basis for the majority of the investments in the company was quite low, I was able to liquidate most holdings at little, if any, loss.

This was of little comfort. The value of the investment had swung from one extreme to the other and my failure to recognize the seriousness of the situation produced a very disappointing outcome.

The Principle of Polarity tells us that everything has its opposite; success and failure are two sides of the same coin. They are both instructive experiences, although failure is far more effective at getting our attention by increasing our receptivity to new insights and opposing points of view. What lessons did I learn from this agonizing experience?

First, as Mark Twain is alleged to have said: "The art of prophecy is very difficult, especially with respect to the future." This is certainly true when it comes to evaluating the truth of information provided by a company's management. After many years of following the company, including many one-to-one discussions with top management, I considered their integrity to be quite high. Being forced to acknowledge fallibility in judging people is certainly disheartening but has its beneficial side effects. I have become more tolerant toward the mistakes of others and my compassion for the human predicament, wherein all souls are enrolled in a difficult and demanding school, has been enhanced. It is said that in circles where Hermes passes, tolerance reigns,[9] and, as I have learned, compassion and tolerance go hand in hand. Moreover, I have come to the realization, as painful and paradoxical as it may seem, that all mistakes are purposeful. They help deflate our egos, appreciate life's apparent imperfections, and intensify our search for meaning in all experiences.

Second, in a world characterized by a minimum of change, analytic skills are quite satisfactory. But, in the warp speed world of high technology, innovation is sudden and often revolutionary and, as such, difficult to analyze in advance. Under such circumstances, non-analytic or intuitive insights are often a more reliable basis for decision making. It is not easy in our scientifically oriented Western culture, to rely on soft or partial information. This difficulty is compounded when the right decision is counter to the consensus. Most security analysts continued to recommend JWP until close to the end. Given the company's history of favorable operating and investment results, it was easier to go along with the "experts" than to take a contrary position. Nonetheless, had I paid more attention to my intuition and less to my rationalizations, I believe I would have made a more appropriate decision.

Third, I now see that the more important a concept is to someone's self-esteem and sense of worth (I wanted to believe I could find the holy grail) the more tenacious he or she will be in defending dubious information and the more likely to reject evidence which conflicts with his or her beliefs. Cultivating a detached view of all outcomes always aids the decision making process. Mistakes can be humbling but, to the extent they prevent future misjudgments, tremendously enlightening.

There are numerous examples of adversity preceding a successful outcome. R. H. Macy failed numerous times before his department store in New York succeeded. Robert M. Pirsig, author of the classic *Zen and the Art of Motorcycle Maintenance* was turned down by 121 publishers before one lone editor gave him a chance. Abraham Lincoln had half a dozen political defeats before being elected President of the United States. While no one looks forward to the pain of failure, such an experience may ultimately lead to a pleasurable outcome. A little sacrifice now may produce enhanced well-being in the future. As we evolve we learn to postpone immediate gratification and sublimate our lower needs to our higher nature. Abraham H. Maslow, one of the founders of humanistic psychology, formalized the concept of hierarchical needs. Maslow arranged his hierarchy into the following five categories:

1. Physical Needs
2. Safety and Security Needs
3. Love and Belongingness
4. Self-Esteem
5. Self-Actualization[10]

Lower and higher have no moral connotations attached to them. Lower needs, such as food (category 1) and protection from predators (category 2) must be satisfied before those that follow in the hierarchy become paramount. A starving person concentrates his time and energy on finding food before worrying about a leaky roof, let alone achieving self-fulfillment. Eventually, however, people place less emphasis on the lower needs and more on higher wants and desires, such as the urge to connect with their spiritual essence.

SCARCITY AND ABUNDANCE

Under circumstances where superficial appearances control our actions, we are led to the conclusion that the resources needed for survival and well-being are limited. In fact, our current economic system is predominately based on this belief. The definition of economics, found in the traditional textbooks, is as follows:

> Economics is the study of how men and society choose, with or without the use of money, to employ **scarce productive resources** [emphasis added] to produce various commodities over time and distribute them for consumption, now and in the future, among various people and groups in society.[11]

With an unlimited desire for the things that bring pleasure and comfort and an apparent scarcity of these resources, it seems reasonable to assume that some desires will go unmet. With not enough to go around, the only way one person can get what he wants is if others make do with less. A competitive mentality follows quite logically from suppositions of scarcity. Moreover, since our status in the community is often enhanced by controlling more resources, the need to acquire these resources becomes an even stronger motivator.[12] What are the fallacies in this logical sounding set of assumptions? We begin with some metaphysical arguments that might be considered soft or ephemeral and conclude with a number of real-life examples, including a statement from one of the most respected and successful businesses in the world.

Based on the Principal of Mentalism, concepts of scarcity are a function of our belief system. The universe, being mental in nature, creates unlimited resources. To quote Elizabeth W. Fenske, Ph.D., Executive Director of Spiritual Frontiers Fellowship International:

> Science is now telling us what metaphysics has expressed down through the ages—that NO THING exists in the universe except energy. This building block of spirit and matter alike is the very source which creates what we perceive outside ourselves and generates all that is within. We draw this energy into our thought processes, and with its help, we create what we want to be the pattern for our lives. This energy knows no boundaries of space or limitations of time. Thought proceeds from this energy and can bring matter into existence and Being. Thus, our power of creativity and human potential is only as limited as we allow it to be.[13]

The Buddha made this succinct comment about the mental foundation of our being:

> We are what we think.
> All that we are arises with our thoughts.
> With our thoughts we make the world.[14]

Many biblical passages confirm the notion that we have the innate power to attract the resources necessary to satisfy all our needs. Two passages from the Gospels of Matthew and Luke are cited below:

> Ask, and it will be given you; seek, and you will find; knock, and it will be opened to you.[15]

> And do not seek what you are to eat and what you are to drink, nor be of anxious mind. Instead, seek his kingdom, and these things shall be yours as well.[16]

Finally, a quote from Paramahansa Yogananda, one of the people most responsible for bringing yoga to the Western world:

> Just as all power lies in His will, so all spiritual and material gifts flow from His boundless abundance. In order to receive His gifts you must eradicate from your *mind* [emphasis added] all thoughts of limitation and poverty. Universal Mind is perfect and knows no lack; to reach that never-failing supply you must maintain a consciousness of abundance. Even when you do not know where the next dollar is coming from, you should refuse to be apprehensive. When you do your part and rely on God to do His, you will find that mysterious forces come to your aid and that your constructive wishes soon materialize.[17]

While the above citations come from well-respected sources, the pragmatist is likely to require more concrete examples before conceding the fact that limited resources are more a mental construct than an actual reality. To that end, the following examples are presented.

The 1798 publication of *An Essay on the Principle of Population*, by Thomas Malthus, raised the fear that the rate of growth in the world's population would outstrip humanity's ability to provide adequate nourishment for its future inhabitants. To Malthus, the economic realities of scarcity and overpopulation appeared so terrifying that he believed wars, famines, and plagues might be the only things saving us from extinction. Many cutting-edge thinkers of that era bought into Malthus' conclusions.[18] As recently as 1968, Paul R. Ehrlich echoed Malthus' fears with a book entitled *The Population Bomb*. In the book he predicted that the world would undergo severe famines in the 1970s and that hundreds of millions of people would starve to death, regardless of any effort to avoid such a tragedy. He also stated that India was a country with such an overwhelming problem trying to feed its population that achieving self-sufficiency would be well-nigh unattainable.[19] Today India no longer needs to import food and is, in fact, emerging as a major food exporter. According to some experts, India has the ability to rival agricultural superpowers such as the United States, Australia and South Africa in the reasonably near future.[20] Both Malthus and Ehrlich failed to take into account our ability to make creative adaptations. With better farm management and the introduction of new technology, we have been able to produce an increasing quantity of food with fewer people. Despite these advances, we readily admit that starvation has been far from eradicated and the world would certainly be better off if population growth were under greater control. Nonetheless, it seems clear that an inadequate supply of food is primarily a consequence of our inability to find more intelligent and innovative answers to the production problem. Food scarcity is essentially a mental problem.

Close behind food, in the list of essentials, is our need for fuel. Fuel keeps the populace warm and provides the power for everything from illumination to locomotion. Since our prehistoric ancestors first pulled burning logs from a lightning-generated fire, we have been finding better and cheaper sources of fuel. Throughout history there has been periodic concern that depletion of the earth's resources would lead to a scarcity of fuel which would eventually impair our standard of living. The most recent episode occurred in the mid-1970s when an Arab oil embargo created an atmosphere of crisis proportions. The price of oil and gas skyrocketed with oil jumping from three dollars to over thirty dollars a barrel and natural gas following commensurably behind. The disastrous consequences that can result from artificially reducing the supply of an essential natural resource became patently obvious. Prices rose dramatically and forecasts of fifty to one hundred dollar a barrel oil were predicted, almost uniformly, by the experts. In fact, as recently as 1981, Frank Zarb, administrator of the now defunct Federal Energy Administration, told a Senate energy subcommittee that oil prices would rise from the then current thirty-six dollars a barrel to one hundred dollars a barrel by 1985. This would result in four dollar a gallon gasoline in 1985 and, according to Zarb, would mean prices reaching well over ten dollars a gallon by the year 2000.[21] Since natural gas has about one-sixth the British Thermal Unit (BTU) equivalent of oil, prices of gas were expected to rise to between eight and sixteen dollars per thousand cubic feet (MCF). What has actually happened since the 1980s? Oil has generally traded below twenty-five dollars per barrel and natural gas has largely remained at or below three dollars per MCF (equivalent to far less than half this amount when adjusted for inflation). Why would two obviously scarce resources not have followed the logical path to substantially higher prices? Technology in the form of more advanced drilling methods and new seismic techniques, better management such as just-in-time delivery and more efficient use of energy in cars and appliances have enabled consumers to use more yet pay less. By unlocking our creative energies, both logic and the experts have been proven resoundingly wrong. According to Carl Wesemann, an independent financial consultant, "The key to finding nature's secrets and using this knowledge in the continuing quest to provide man an inexhaustible energy source lies in the **mind** [emphasis added] of man himself."[22]

Peter Drucker, renowned author, teacher and management consultant, has spoken about how people are increasingly being paid for the sole purpose of putting knowledge to work. The transformation from working with one's hands to one's mind is the biggest change ever for mankind, according to Drucker.[23] This idea is seconded by Virginia I. Postrel, editor of *Reason* magazine. In an article entitled, "It's All In The Head," she states:

> We are, in fact, living more and more in an *intangible* economy, in which the greatest sources of wealth are not physical. We aren't yet used to an economy in which beauty, amusement, attention, learning, pleasure, even spiritual fulfillment are as real and economically valuable as steel or semiconductors. . . . The intangible economy, . . . [creates] something valuable out of the most abundant and insubstantial of raw materials—out of thought itself.[24]

In an effort to conclude this discussion on scarcity versus abundance with "hard" evidence from the real world, there could be nothing better than the following passage from an Annual Report of the General Electric Company:

> Increasing our competitiveness is at the heart of all this "soft stuff"—boundaryless behavior, increasing our speed and stretch, with an overlay of simplification. And the excitement they produce is, obviously, in the hard results they generate, but even more importantly, it is in the knowledge that what we have done *has barely scratched the surface.* It turns out that there is, in fact, unlimited juice in that lemon. The fact is that none of this is about squeezing anything at all—it is about tapping an ocean of creativity, passion and energy that, as far as we can see, has no bottom and no shores.
>
> Using 100% of the **minds** [emphasis added] and passion of 100% of our people in implementing the best ideas from everywhere in the world is a formula, we believe, for endless excitement, endless growth and endless renewal.[25]

Finally, the words of Yogi Berra, the Hall of Fame catcher and manager of the New York Yankees and Mets, should go a long way in quieting any remaining skeptics. In a speech at the graduation ceremony of Montclair State University in Montclair, New Jersey, Berra said: "Remember that whatever you do in life, ninety percent of it is mental." While his statement still leaves ten percent in dispute, one should also take into account that at the same function he was heard to state: ". . . during the years ahead, when you come to a fork in the road, take it."[26]

SEPARATE AND UNEQUAL

The illusion that each of us is separate and autonomous is a common one and follows directly from reliance on our senses. We see only an indirect and tenuous connection to our fellow human beings and the natural world that surrounds us. When we view ourselves as separate with little connection to others, we assume our interests are best served by competing rather than cooperating. This separative belief is reinforced by the cultural mores and traditions of the society we inherit. Charles T. Tart, psychology professor and author of *Waking Up: Overcoming the Obstacles to Human Potential*, describes the situation as follows:

> Cultures almost never encourage their members to question them. Physical survival has been too precarious for too many people for most of our history, so there is a deep, if implicit, feeling that our culture has kept us alive in a rough world; don't ask questions, don't rock the boat. Cultures try to be closed systems.[27]

When the mind automatically regurgitates the opinions and values of the culture, a state of mass mind or consensus trance is achieved. Some commonly held beliefs include:

- Foreigners have strange beliefs.
- Over there is better than over here.
- I have no responsibility for society's poverty, pollution or educational problems.
- I would be happy if I had what my neighbor just bought.
- If I were more like them I would have greater acceptance.
- I know what is best for them.
- My belief system is free of any distortions or conditioning.

Most, if not all, of these beliefs can be tied to the fact that we feel we are separate entities. As such, we act as if our thoughts and actions can be pursued without considering how they may impact others. How do we break free of the inhibiting and destructive beliefs that have been implanted into our psyches since childhood?

Ageless wisdom, it will be recalled, teaches that a key to enlightenment is to "Know Thyself." Self-knowledge helps us see that our separative thinking and selfish behavior are causing us pain and need to be reversed. Professor Jacob Needleman expresses it this way, "The other world, the world of the spirit, is approached through the increase of attention in oneself, through consciousness of oneself in the midst of hell. The awareness of hell is the escape from hell, or the beginning of the escape."[28] Through a combination of keen observation and probing experimentation, like the alchemists of old, we learn that we are not separate as our senses would have us believe. The body is only the outer covering, the costume or mask for our soul which is united with all other souls. The idea that all souls are ultimately united is in keeping with the Principle of Mentalism, which describes a universe of unbroken conscious energy interpenetrating everything in existence.

Self-observation involves shifting one's center of consciousness from the one who desires and acts to the detached observer of one's thoughts, emotions, motivations and actions. From this position it is easier to determine the extent to which our activities are based on unconscious habits and mass mind thinking rather than well-reasoned, discriminating choices. Only by looking at the causes behind our desires will we begin to want what we truly need. To do otherwise can result in our getting what we wanted only to find out what we got is not what we expected.

To summarize, we have been looking at a stage of development in which humans believe themselves to be separate and autonomous beings. From this belief system flow a number of mistakes which aid in the evolutionary process. All of the pairs of opposites are experienced, life after life, until one realizes that the pairs are only different aspects of the same thing. Rather than being separate, everything is connected. Rather than being materially based, the universe is all mental. By changing our mental framework anything and everything becomes possible. As we change, so must the organizations for which we work. Unless the institutions and organizations around which today's social and commercial activities are centered reflect this new way of thinking, individuals will become frustrated and lack motivation. Thomas Jefferson, in a letter to Samuel Kercheval, remarks on the need for institutional changes as the human mind progresses:

I am certainly not an advocate for frequent changes in laws and constitutions. . . . But I know also, that laws and institutions must go hand in hand with the progress of the human mind. As that becomes more developed, more enlightened, as new discoveries are made, new truths discovered and manners and opinions change with the change of circumstances, institutions must advance also to keep pace with the times. We might as well require a man to wear still the coat which fitted him when a boy, as civilized society to remain ever under the regimen of their barbarous ancestors.[29]

It will become more evident, in the ensuing chapters, that businesses are beginning to make the changes that are necessary to keep pace with the expanding number of their employees who are embracing a more holistic worldview. As teachings such as the Hermetic Principles gain wider acceptance, society will have a guiding ethic and a transformation model for the twenty-first century.

NOTES

1. Anna Kennedy Winner. *The Basic Ideas of Occult Wisdom* (Wheaton, IL: The Theosophical Publishing House, 1970), pp. 83–91.

2. Ken Keyes, Jr. *Handbook to Higher Consciousness* (Berkeley, CA: Living Love Center, 1973), pp. 11–14.

3. Willis W. Harman. *Global Mind Change: The Promise of the Last Years of the Twentieth Century* (Indianapolis: Knowledge Systems, Inc. for the Institute of Noetic Sciences, 1988), pp. 11–14.

4. Barbara Brennan. *Light Emerging* (New York: Bantam Books, 1993), p. 33.

5. Winner, pp. 88–89.

6. Paul A. Samuelson. *Economics: An Introductory Analysis*, 6th ed. (New York: McGraw-Hill Book Co., 1964), p. 24.

7. Elliot Markowitz. "Dwyer Claims JWP Down but Not Out," *Computer Reseller News*, 26 October 1992, p. 221.

8. Floyd Norris. "Market Place," *New York Times*, 22 September 1995, p. 6(D).

9. Faivre, p. 100.

10. Charles T. Tart. *Waking Up: Overcoming the Obstacles to Human Potential*, New Science Library (Boston: Shambhala Publications, 1986), p. 173.

11. Samuelson, p. 5.

12. Denise Breton and Christopher Largent. *The Soul of Economies: Spiritual Evolution Goes to the Marketplace* (Wilmington, DE: Idea House Publishing Co., 1991), pp. 83–85.

13. Elizabeth W. Fenske, ed. "Creativity and Human Potential," *Spiritual Insights for Daily Living* (Independence, MO: Independence Press for Spiritual Frontiers Fellowship, 1986), June.

14. T. Byrom, *The Dhammapada: The Sayings of the Buddha* (New York: Vintage, 1976), quoted in Roger N. Walsh and Frances Vaughan, eds. *Beyond Ego: Transpersonal Dimensions in Psychology* (Los Angeles: Jeremy P. Tarcher, 1980), p. 58.

15. Matthew 7:7 (Revised Standard Version).

16. Luke 12:29, 12:31 (Revised Standard Version).

17. Paramahansa Yogananda. *The Law of Success*, 7th ed. (Los Angeles: Self-Realization Fellowship, 1983), p. 22.

18. Thomas Robert Malthus. *On Population*, ed. Gertrude Himmelfarb, The Modern Library (New York: Random House, 1960), p. 9.

19. Paul Ehrlich. *The Population Bomb* (New York: Ballantine Books, 1968), Prologue, pp. 39–41.

20. Peter Fuhrman and Michael Schuman. "Now We Are Our Own Masters," *Forbes*, 23 May 1994, p. 136.

21. Jim Landers. "Gasoline to Hit $4 per Gallon, Specialist Says," *Dallas Morning News*, 2 May 1981, p. 1(A).

22. Carl Wesemann. "The Primary Energy Source, or, Food for Thought," in *Energy Sources 78/79*, ed. Rita Blome (Denver: ENERCOM, 1978), p. 26.

23. Gerard A. Achstatter. "Prescription for Success: Change Fast —and Often," *Investor's Business Daily*, 2 May 1996, p. 4(A).

24. Virginia I. Postrel. "It's All in the Head," *Forbes ASAP*, 26 February 1996, p. 118. Reprinted by permission of *Forbes ASAP* Magazine © Forbes Inc. 1996.

25. General Electric Company. *1994 Annual Report* (Fairfield, CT), p. 5. Used with permission.

26. William H. Honan. "Of Spielberg, Berra and (Many) Other Graduation Greats," *New York Times*, 17 May 1996, p. 6(B). Copyright © 1996 by The New York Times Co. Reprinted by permission.

27. Tart, p. 88.

28. Jacob Needleman. *Money and the Meaning of Life* (New York: Doubleday, a division of Bantam Doubleday Dell Publishing Group, 1991), p. 171.

29. J. G. De Roulhac Hamilton, ed. *The Best Letters of Thomas Jefferson* (Cambridge: Riverside Press, 1926), p. 220.

4

The Road to Cooperation

Humanity's adventure, veiled by the illusion of separation, continues until the discomfort reaches intolerable levels. The four errors discussed in the previous chapter place severe limits on our ability to attain a sense of peace and contentment. As long as the ideas of autonomy and scarcity prevail, we find ourselves locked in a maze of win-lose, competitive battles in which we feel less secure and less fulfilled than is our birthright. As Socrates said: "No man starts out to be wise until he sees what it costs him to be a fool."[1] Misguided patterns of conduct are the norm until it is realized that egocentric behavior is counterproductive. Each person's progress, in the school of life, is inextricably tied to the well-being of everything else. When individuals start thinking in terms of Willis Harman's second metaphysic, which moves from materialistic monism (M-1) to dualism (M-2), the atmosphere starts to change. Humanity shifts from believing that matter is primary toward two equal and complementary ways of viewing the world. One is composed of matter-energy stuff and the other mind-spirit stuff.[2] Neither the idea that all things are interconnected nor that we live in a world of unlimited potential are evident when thinking is restricted to a materialistic structure. When mind is put on an equal footing with matter, our idea of what is possible transcends the limitations of the physical senses and we begin to imagine the intangible bonds that have been hidden. By changing the focus from separate to connected and from scarce to abundant, we move from a dependence on competition and coercion to an understanding that competition is just one way of interacting; in many cases, it is neither the most productive nor the most satisfying.

One obvious alternative to competition is cooperation. Here the parties involved work together with the intention of achieving a common goal. Competition is not necessarily eliminated, for it can provide a spark that raises the energy level of all participants and helps avoid the tendency toward complacency or a herd mentality. Competition is simply relegated to a secondary role so that the goal is more broadly defined and disruptive conflict is minimized.[3] For those who believe large scale cooperative efforts are an idealistic dream, a number of examples will show how this mode of connecting can be more productive and fulfilling than the inordinately restrictive competitive model that currently dominates most relationships.

REFLECTIONS FROM NATURE

Simple yet effective cooperative arrangements are seen most keenly in the non-human world where behaviors stem from unconscious, instinctive impulses. Absent free will, most actions are spontaneous and generally in harmony with universal laws and principles. What are some of the characteristics that dominate the natural world? Nature seems to thrive on cooperation and abhor competition. It disperses organisms geographically, by livelihood, and by territory. Except when trying to win a mate, territorial encounters among various animals are not really forms of competition but purposeful displays and gestures in which the challenger is trying to find out if the territory is taken. With a few exceptions, the only time there is a fight to the death is when a predator's subsistence or safety is dependent upon it. Supposedly civilized people, however, have engaged in killing purely for "sport" for a long time. Some might consider this type of action an outgrowth of competitiveness reaching an irresponsible extreme. Most Native Americans, for instance, were closely aligned with nature's ways and condemned killing simply for the fun of it. In 1854, Chief Seattle, leader of the combined Ouwamish and Suquamish tribes, wrote a letter to President Franklin Pierce that touched on his tribes' view of man's dependence on the natural environment:

> I have seen a thousand rotting buffalo on the prairie, left by the white man who shot them from a passing train. I am a savage and do not understand how the smoking Iron Horse can be more important than the buffalo that we will kill only to stay alive. What is man without the beasts? If all the beasts were gone, man would die from a great loneliness of spirit. For whatever happens to the beasts, soon happens to man. All things are connected.[4]

Cooperation among and within species is also quite prevalent. Consider the following example of inter-species cooperation. An animal eats a fruit, seed and all. Later the animal deposits the undigested seeds with a good amount of fertilizer. The animal is fed and a new fruit tree is soon generated. Even byproducts are used to support life among species. Animals need oxygen to breathe; plants provide that. Plants need carbon dioxide which, conveniently, is a byproduct of animals' breathing.

The cleaning symbiosis is another example of cooperation among species. Whether it is the rhinoceros bird picking insects off the rhino's back or one of the forty-two species of fish that specialize in cleaning other fish, animals are often found working together. In truth, no species could exist if it were alone on the planet.[5] We recycle for one another. A vivid memory of a visit to the African plains was the total absence of trash or waste anywhere; one species' waste was another species' nutriments. Humans are just beginning to understand the consequences of their woefully deficient recycling efforts. The respectful, codependent interaction among non-human species is a clear example of cooperative relationships that directly benefit the participants.

Humanity's interdependence with all of creation becomes less deniable the closer one looks. When the Pacific sea otter had been hunted to the brink of extinction at the turn of the century, populations of eagles, harbor seals and, of most immediate concern to man, fish fell dramatically. It turned out that kelp, part of a complicated food chain, was being cut loose by sea urchins whose primary predator was the sea otter. Without the kelp to nourish the marine life that sustains the fish population which in turn supports the eagles and seals, all of these species declined to dangerous levels. With the otter population depleted, the chain disintegrated to the detriment of not only the plants and animals in the chain but humans as well.[6] As stated by John C. Sawhill, of the Nature Conservancy, "I often compare the natural world to an enormous tapestry, marvelous in its complexity and interdependence. With each extinction of another species, we pull another thread out of that tapestry."[7]

Nature has much to teach us; one of the most important lessons is that the same ripple effects that occur in nature are also found in our political and financial lives. The Mexican financial crisis of 1994 provided a striking example of humanity's irrefutable interdependence. A surprise year-end devaluation of the peso caught most investors by surprise and securities markets from Brazil to Hong Kong were sent spinning. In today's global economy there are virtually no barriers to the free flow of capital. The combined stock market capitalization of Latin America, Asia and Africa has grown from around $100 billion ten years ago to well over $2 trillion.[8] Investors are from all regions of the world and include both individuals, many of whom invest through mutual funds, and financial institutions. The latter are often managing the retirement funds of not only wealthy but less affluent pensioners as well. Thus when a crisis, real or imagined, develops, everyone is affected regardless of nationality or ability to sustain loss.

The Mexican crisis mentioned above was of such magnitude that the June 1997 Denver Summit of the Eight, led by President Clinton, placed avoidance of similar financial crises high on its agenda. It was none too soon. If there was ever a question about the world's interdependence it was quickly laid to rest by late 1997. Financial turmoil in Asia, starting with Thailand and Malaysia and then spreading to Indonesia, Hong Kong, Korea and Japan, pointed up the need for close consultation and cooperation among countries worldwide. With several countries near bankruptcy and numerous multinational corporations defaulting on loans, International Monetary Fund rescue packages were quickly put in place to try and contain the crisis and restore confidence. The United States and much of Europe faced undesirable repercussions in spite of the prevalence of strong economic fundamentals. By 1998 it was clear that worldwide growth would, at best, be stultified. Depressed currencies enabled Asian countries to flood Western markets with cheap imports, thereby reducing domestic economic growth and threatening job markets. Regardless of culpability, no country goes unscathed when any nation faces a crisis. What applies to financial crises also holds true when lax pollution detection or enforcement permits harmful emissions in the air or water. Just as capital and information flows are not inhibited by geographical or political borders, neither are the effects of environmental degradation.

SURVIVAL OF THE COOPERATIVE

Darwin's theory of the survival of the fittest rightly points out that creatures who are best able to adapt to changing conditions are the ones most likely to survive and perpetuate the species. In the same manner, the socioeconomic prototype that facilitates the most creative adaptations is the one that will endure. According to Alfie Kohn, author of *No Contest: The Case against Competition* and recipient of the National Psychology Award, studies show that cooperation is more effective than competition in effecting necessary adaptations. Kohn says that competition often gets in the way of success. He cites a number of reasons for his seemingly radical position. First, competition causes anxiety. When someone is trying to beat you and you are trying to beat her, it is only natural that both parties become distracted. The focus of attention shifts from the ultimate objective to your competitor's strategy for winning the current phase. Second, competition may be less efficient than cooperation. In a competitive battle, skills and resources are hoarded for fear of losing an advantage to an opponent. Therefore, competition can be wasteful and redundant. Furthermore, at some point one of the opposing sides is likely to be wasting time and energy fixing problems that have already been solved. Third, competition diverts attention from the task at hand to the goal of winning at any cost.

The emotional and egotistical goals that we try to satisfy in our competitive encounters are often thwarted as our self-esteem becomes dependent on continually beating someone or winning at some activity. Intrinsic motivations, such as curiosity or satisfaction from a job well done, are undermined. Too often what may have started out as exciting becomes less appealing as the stress and anxiety brought on by competitive pressure take their toll. Finally, competition can poison personal relationships. Competitors are conditioned to be less trusting and less sensitive to other people's needs or points of view.[9] As we come to understand that consciousness, rather than physicality, is the essence of our being, the compulsion to compete for scarce resources diminishes.

A PRACTICAL APPLICATION

Few people would disagree that society's mechanisms for settling disputes, either between individuals or institutions, leave much to be desired. Courts are backlogged with far too many cases and the expense of litigating conflicts, particularly in the United States, borders on the absurd. Total costs of the tort system in America were estimated by Tillinghast, an international consulting firm, at over $150 billion or approximately 2.2 percent of the U.S. gross domestic product. Figures compiled for eleven other industrialized countries showed that litigation costs in these countries were only 0.9 percent of gross domestic product. The difference is approximately nine hundred dollars per United

States household. These outlandish expenses get reflected in higher than "normal" prices for goods and services such as automobiles and insurance premiums.[10] Besides higher costs, even the eventual "winner" can be worse off than when the dissension first surfaced. There clearly has to be a better way. Setting the proper tone at the outset of a relationship may be a key to limiting lengthy confrontations.

A novel legal agreement, which was brought to my attention many years ago with regard to a personal investment, sets the stage for a more congenial atmosphere at the outset. A small but essential part of the agreement, in modified form, follows:

> The parties know that in all human endeavors disputes can occur. In an effort to maintain long, mutually satisfying relationships the undersigned desire to minimize the time, money and aggravation spent settling any misunderstanding. Furthermore, the parties want the dispute resolution process to be one that is mutually educational; one that enables all parties to learn about their respective feelings and thought processes so that disagreements can be settled in a friendly, detached manner. In addition, the parties want to avoid lengthy and disruptive court proceedings that often result in the litigants being so upset and disaffected that the chance for future dealings are jeopardized. To this end the parties agree to settle any dispute in a series of stages so that disagreements will be detected and resolved at the earliest possible time. Therefore, anytime a feeling of discomfort arises, for any reason whatsoever, the aggrieved party will immediately communicate that concern as specifically as possible. The party that is the alleged cause of the discomfort shall willingly discuss the matter and the parties involved will do whatever they can to eliminate the problem. There shall be no assertions of blame or fault as it is the undersigned's intention to cooperate in such a manner that the disagreement is expeditiously resolved.[11]

Even with the best of intentions, some disagreements will not be settled at this initial stage. Therefore, additional steps requiring a more involved engagement would need to be promulgated in any formal agreement. We are not, of course, attempting to present a comprehensive legal document. Our objective is simply to show that when parties set an amicable tone and affirm an intention to remain civil and cooperative disputes have a better chance of being settled quickly and easily. As John Rutledge, economist and chairman of a merchant bank, sees it: "Allowing your opponent in a transaction to walk away with his dignity, his humor and his hearing intact, and a pretty good deal in his pocket, is the right way to do business."[12]

FROM ECONOMIC THEORY

Adam Smith, the patron saint of modern economics, published his groundbreaking book, *The Wealth of Nations*, in 1776. In it he wrote:

> In civilized society he stands at all times in need of the **cooperation** [emphasis added] and assistance of great multitudes, while his whole life is scarce sufficient to gain the friendship of a few persons. . . . But man has almost constant occasion for the help of his brethren, and it is in vain for him to expect it from their benevolence only. He will be more likely to prevail if he can interest their self-love in his favour, and shew [*sic*] them that it is for their own advantage to do for him what he requires of them. Give me that which I want, and you shall have this which you want, is the meaning of every such offer; and it is in this manner that we obtain from one another the far greater part of those good offices which we stand in need of.[13]

Later in the treatise he states:

> . . . he is in this, as in many other cases, led by an invisible hand to promote an end which was no part of his intention. Nor is it always the worse for the society that it was no part of it. By pursuing his own interest he frequently promotes that of the society more effectually than when he really intends to promote it.[14]

We need each others' help. If we show others that it is in their best interest to help us, they will. Life is more rewarding and productive both when we obtain help from others and offer help in return. Over time, enlightened self-interest changes self-love into cooperation; given our interdependence, such a metamorphosis enriches the common good.

TO PRAGMATIC BUSINESS

Business and competition have been thought of as virtually synonymous for a long time. With the dramatic advances in telecommunications via computers, fax machines, wireless telephony, the Internet, etc., citizens of the world have grown much closer together and business leaders have begun altering some former views about how to conduct their operations. As John Naisbitt states in his book *Global Paradox*:

> Competition and cooperation have become the yin and yang of the global marketplace. Like yin and yang they are always seeking balance and always changing. Competition we know about. One thrust of the new cooperation, the new strategic alliances, is to carve out a piece of your world in which you agree to cooperate with your strongest competitor who very much remains your competitor.[15]

As an example of a cooperative strategic alliance between traditional rivals, consider a California-based firm by the name of General Magic. A partnership originally formed among international giants Apple Computer, AT&T, Matsushita Electric, Motorola, Philips and Sony, it is involved in making communications easier and more productive. According to Joanna Hoffman, of General Magic:

> Ten years ago, we were in our 20s and the industry was very different. We never gave a thought to cooperate. We were going to take over the world. . . . Today, the industry is far more complex. There is a web of relationships in which companies cooperate and compete at the same time.[16]

The world of goods and services procurement offers a good illustration of what can be accomplished by cooperative arrangements. Customers treating their suppliers like their own employees was almost unheard of until recently. JIT II, the 1990s version of just-in-time inventory control, is designed to create harmony and efficiency between customer and supplier. Sharing such things as up-to-the-minute sales forecasts, JIT II relies on mutual trust. Often there is initial concern on both sides about releasing too much in the way of confidential information or technological secrets. It is always possible that an in-house supplier might overhear conversations about a competitor's prices. Conversely, suppliers may be asked to reveal their costs. But the benefits of being able to reduce supplies, eliminate redundant inventory and get cost-saving tips from a more informed supplier usually outweigh the possible problems.

Honeywell's Golden Valley Minnesota factory has had fifteen representatives from ten suppliers, ranging from printed materials to electronics, occupy their own workspace near the production floor. In overseeing purchases for existing products, they try to think like a Honeywell employee, constantly searching for ways to trim costs. Honeywell's results include inventory levels measured in days rather than months, 25 percent fewer purchasing agents, and suggestions on ways to standardize some parts so they are easier to make. While suppliers are given considerable freedom to order inventory, misuse of this authority could jeopardize not only Honeywell's business but the suppliers' reputations as well. While these cooperative efforts have not been successful in every instance, many large corporations are getting on the bandwagon and experimenting with these forward looking arrangements.[17]

PUBLIC RELATIONS AND PRIVATE COMMITMENT

In general, corporate literature and advertising are quick to tout the ways their company is encouraging a cooperative culture. For some this appears to be no more than a thinly disguised attempt to garner positive public relations. In other cases it seems to have deeper roots as it reflects a genuine reappraisal of the business environment. General Motors, for instance, claims to have embraced the cooperative spirit on a number of fronts. Along with Ford and Chrysler, GM has entered into research and development arrangements with the federal government to produce the next generation of vehicles. This partnership brings together the resources of the U.S. National Laboratories, many universities, and the domestic auto manufacturers and suppliers for the purpose of making the technological breakthroughs needed for improved fuel economy. Additional cooperative, industry-government projects are underway in other areas of socially beneficial, pre-competitive research and development. A recent GM Annual Report emphatically states: "We believe these cooperative efforts will prove to be much more effective in achieving the nation's vehicle safety and environmental and energy goals than the often contentious and frustrating 'command-and-control' regulatory approach of the last 25 years." They go on to declare: "We are serious about this new emphasis on cooperation." To reinforce this claim they list numerous educational and environmental organizations with which they are actively engaged.[18] The breadth of their commitment is impressive. With the strict accountability required by several of their partners, it seems reasonable to give GM the benefit of the doubt and assume their intentions are sincere.

Cable and Wireless plc (CWP) is a large multinational corporation. Serving customers in over fifty countries on five continents, its stock is quoted on eight international stock exchanges. The company helped lay the first successful Transatlantic telegraph cable in the 1860s and by 1900 had connected five continents. With some 40 percent of their forty thousand person workforce in the Asian Pacific, 28 percent in the United Kingdom and Europe and 24 percent in the Caribbean, they have a truly international perspective. Such a geographical diversification also gives them a good sense of the world's interdependence and undoubtedly accounts for the following view: "Being 'out there in the world' for so long bred a sense of cooperation and partnership into Cable and Wireless people—and that is now one of the Group's most enduring strengths." They believe teamwork is their most valued tradition; it undoubtedly was a catalyst for their decision to set up Cable and Wireless College. With a teaching staff of seventy, one of its primary objectives is to bond their multinational and multicultural federation together so that the company can create a learning network all over the world. They enthusiastically embrace the idea of working collaboratively with other organizations. CWP has more than fifty partners including a dozen governments, many local companies and over twenty-five other telecommunications groups.[19] It seems fair to conclude that the more international exposure a company has, the greater their inclination to work cooperatively with their employees, customers and competitors.

COOPERATIVE VIBRATIONS

Establishing cooperative arrangements is a natural outgrowth of the belief that everything is interconnected and, therefore, interdependent. The Hermetic Principle of Vibration tells us that the only difference among the myriad objects we identify through our senses is the rate at which they vibrate. As discussed in chapter two, there is a universal substance that pervades all space and serves as a medium of transmission. It joins all forms of vibrating energy including those which manifest as physical matter. In addition, every mental state is composed of vibrations. Thus, nothing we do or think stands in isolation. The Principle of Vibration further states that the vibrational frequency (number of periodic oscillations) of any object produces a signal. Once emitted, the signal is drawn to objects vibrating at a similar frequency, thereby connecting like thoughts and emotions.[20] This principle may be the basis for activating various psychic functions (psi). Psychic perception is thought to encompass three classes: telepathy (mind-to-mind communication), clairvoyance (perception of current events, objects or people that are hidden from the five senses) and precognition (knowledge of future events that cannot be perceived by any known means).[21] The United States government supported psi research at SRI International (formerly Stanford Research Institute) for more than a decade, beginning in the 1970s. An excerpt from the 1981 report of a Congressional committee made what, to many, seemed like a startling conclusion:

> Recent experiments in remote viewing and other studies in parapsychology suggest that there is an "interconnectedness" of the human mind with other minds and matter. . . . Experiments on mind-mind interconnectedness have yielded some encouraging results. . . . The implications of these experiments is that the human mind may be able to obtain information independent of geography and time.[22]

Because everything is intertwined through a medium of vibrating energy, mentally attuning ourselves to the vibration rate of an object enables us to gain information that transcends "normal" time and space limitations. Developing a higher level of intuitive awareness leads to penetrating the boundaries that seem to separate us from the planet's many inhabitants. We permeate nature and are permeated by it. To the extent we become conscious participants with nature, our psychic abilities are enhanced. Russell Targ and Keith Harary describe how we exercise our psychic abilities as follows:

> What we are reaching for is not above or beyond us, but within us. It is not "higher," but deeper. It lies not in the narrow answers we sometimes give ourselves about what life means, but in the deeper questions we are asking ourselves about who we are. It is the part of us that remembers its participation in a larger community of humanity and nature—the part of us that is psychic.[23]

Control and manipulation of the vibratory rate of matter may be the secret to the "miracles" found in the Bible and elsewhere.

The bestseller, *Mutant Message Downunder*, created a great deal of controversy, in part at least, because it describes how an Australian Aborigine miraculously healed a broken bone.[24] It is difficult to validate this story but the healing discussed in the book seems to be in accord with other metaphysical discussions of healing various parts of the anatomy. Moreover, scientists now seem to understand the intricacies of bone healing at the cellular level. Robert Becker, an orthopedic surgeon and researcher, spent many years proving that tiny electrical currents generated at the site of an injury cause cells at the edges of a fracture to revert from their mature condition to an earlier state where they have a higher capacity for growth and regeneration. These primitive cells recoup potentials mature cells have lost. This has led him to look beyond bones to other types of healing, such as the extraordinary ability of salamanders to regenerate amputated limbs. Becker concluded that limb regeneration in salamanders is fundamentally the same as bone healing in humans and, at least in theory, humans should have the same ability. In essence all the needed circuitry and apparatus is present; the problem is simply to discover how to turn on the right switches to activate the process.[25] Mystics maintain that if we learn to raise our own vibrational levels the healing process can be "miraculously" accelerated.

To recapitulate, we evolve from a state where everything appears separate and inadequate, to a stage where we recognize that we are firmly linked together and able to secure all we need. Because everything is part of a universal substance (analogous perhaps to Adam Smith's "invisible hand"), we are unalterably bound together; our own interests are maximized when we operate out of a spirit of community and good will. All types of cooperative actions accord with the "forgotten truth" of interdependence. The next chapter takes us further along the spiritual path and in so doing solves the other two problems that arise from a belief in autonomy.

NOTES

1. Daphna Moore. *The Rabbi's Tarot: Spiritual Secrets of the Tarot* (St. Paul, MN: Llewellyn Publications, 1992), p. 272.

2. Harman, p. 34.

3. Cynthia Joba, Herman Bryant Maynard, Jr. and Michael Ray. "Competition, Cooperation and Co-Creation: Insights From the World Business Academy," in *The New Paradigm in Business: Emerging Strategies for Leadership and Organizational Change,* ed. Michael Ray and Alan Rinzler (New York: Putnam Publishing Group for the World Business Academy, 1993), p. 50.

4. "Can One Sell The Sky? Indian Asks," *Salt Lake Tribune,* 6 June 1976.

5. Robert Augros and George Stanciu. "The New Biology," *Noetic Sciences Review,* Winter 1989, pp. 4–8.

6. John C. Sawhill. "The Tangled Web We Weave," *Nature Conservancy,* May/June 1992, p. 3.

7. Ibid.

8. Karen Pennar. "Why Investors Stampede," *Business Week,* 13 February 1995, p. 85.

9. Alfie Kohn. "The Case Against Competition," *Noetic Sciences Collection 1980 to 1990,* p. 89.

10. Paul H. Rubin. "The High Cost of Lawsuits," *Investor's Business Daily,* 4 March 1996, p. 2(A).

11. *Integrity Agreement, Lawforms Uniform Agreement Establishing Procedures for Settling Disputes,* G-4a LawForms, pp. 4-80, 3-87.

12. John Rutledge. "The Portrait on my Office Wall," *Forbes,* 30 December 1996, p. 78. Reprinted by permission of *Forbes* Magazine © Forbes Inc. 1996.

13. Adam Smith. *An Inquiry into the Nature and Causes of the Wealth of Nations,* ed. with an Introduction and Commentary by Kathryn Sutherland. World Classics (Oxford: Oxford University Press, 1993), p. 22.

14. Ibid, p. 292.

15. John Naisbitt, *Global Paradox* (New York: Avon Books, 1994), p. 13.

16. Ibid, pp. 69–71.

17. Fred R. Bleakley. "Strange Bedfellows," *Wall Street Journal*, 13 January 1995, p. 1(A).

18. General Motors Corporation. *1994 Annual Report* (Detroit, MI), pp. 11–12.

19. Cable and Wireless plc. *1994 Report and Accounts* and *Supplemental Brochure* (London), pp. 7, 20.

20. Norma Milanovich and Shirley McCune. *The Light Shall Set You Free* (Albuquerque, NM: Athena Publishing, 1996), p. 207.

21. Russell Targ and Keith Harary. *The Mind Race: Understanding and Using Psychic Abilities*, with a Foreword by Willis Harman. (New York: Villard Books, 1984), p. 53.

22. Ibid, p. 4.

23. Ibid, p. 244.

24. Marlo Morgan. *Mutant Message Downunder* (Lees Summit, MO: MM Co., 1991), p. 93.

25. Weil, p. 80.

5

The Dawn of Cocreation

Believing that all humanity is connected and acting in a cooperative spirit are giant advances over the worldview that we are all
separate and, therefore, need to engage in win/lose, competitive
clashes. It is not, however, the end of the journey. Willis Harman's metaphysical model points to the next change in our evolution. The M-1 stage, it may be recalled, assumes that everything
arises out of matter. At the M-2 stage, both matter-energy stuff
and mind-spirit stuff coexist as equal but fundamentally different
aspects of reality. Humanity, in general, is now beginning to
think in terms of a M-3 cosmology in which all things are united.[1]
From this perspective, the only thing that exists is consciousness.
All matter—animal, vegetable or mineral—has some degree of
awareness. An M-3 mind-set accepts the view that we are not
only superficially connected but, in fact, an integral part of an infinite, eternal consciousness. Plato expressed this idea quite elo-
quently when he wrote:

> The ruler of the universe has ordered all things with a view to
> the excellence and preservation of the whole, and each part, as
> far as may be, has an action and passion appropriate to it. Over
> these, down to the least fraction of them, ministers have been

appointed to preside, who have wrought out their perfection with infinitesimal exactness. And one of these portions of the universe is thine own, unhappy man, which, however little, contributes to the whole; and you do not seem to be aware that this and every other creation is for the sake of the whole, and in order that the life of the whole may be blessed; and that you are created for the sake of the whole, and not the whole for the sake of you.[2]

The reality behind the phenomenal world, as described by Plato and other teachers of esoteric traditions, cannot be known through the physical senses. There is little choice, therefore, but to accept or reject the idea of unity, at least initially, on faith. The sages tell us, however, that the doors to understanding and experiencing the oneness of life will open when the desire is sincere and persistent enough. Glimpses of the ultimate reality are said to be revealed in our dreams and mythology. These states, unfettered by logic and common sense, are full of magic and paradoxical situations. Rich in images and lacking precision, they convey the way mystics experience reality in a manner more real than that communicated by mere language.[3]

The fundamental wisdom contained in dreams has been widely accepted since ancient times by many cultures. It was believed that we learn much about ourselves and our relationship to the universe by attuning to the subjective reality of dreams. Greeks and Romans thought that when the body was asleep the soul became free to travel to nonworldly realms. Plato called this realm the *metaxu*, or "the between." Here the human soul had supernatural experiences and encounters; it was possible to meet the gods, see the future and be healed of illness. Shamanic cultures access dream states for the same purpose; Tibetans uncover information about past lives. Dreams have also been credited with inspiring great creativity. Physicist Neils Bohr had a dream that revealed the model for the atom; nineteenth-century Russian chemist Mendeleev had a vision of the periodic table of elements while asleep. Artist William Blake was given a process for copper engraving in a dream, a technique that enabled him to make a living from his mystical illustrations. Author Robert Louis Stevenson's idea for *The Strange Case of Dr. Jekyll and Mr. Hyde* was revealed in a dream and poet William Taylor Coleridge transcribed part of *Kubla Khan* verbatim from a dream until it was interrupted. The list of creative inspirations from dreams is probably endless; the point, however, was clear to the ancients. They considered revelations contained in dreams to be gifts from the gods. Dreams were thought to be one of the few media whereby divine messages could be relayed to earthly creatures.[4] ·

Many believe that revelations about the nature of ultimate reality are received by certain prophets or messengers who often communicate these new understandings through a reinterpretation of existing symbols. Rather than conveying specific beliefs or dogma, they provide principles for use in evolving ourselves. The intention would seem to be to encourage the reexamination of values and priorities; looking deeply within can have a profound impact on how we lead our lives.[5] Finally, meditative practices are said to enable us to pierce the veil that hides the ineffable beauty, harmony and unity that mystics have long experienced.

For those of us not yet blessed by divine revelation but who still want to understand our place in the universe, The Principle of Correspondence can be of inestimable help. As may be recalled, there is analogy and agreement among all forms of manifestation. What is true of amoebae is true of humans and beings more evolved. What is true of matter is true of energy and mind. Thus the whole can be understood by studying its parts just as solar systems can be known by examining atoms and molecules.[6]

Pictorial, or non-language, symbols are used and understood across cultures and serve as representations of the correspondences between planes of existence. Many of these ancient symbols, which can activate subconscious responses, correspond to archetypal concepts that are operative throughout the macrocosm. According to Carl G. Liungman, author of the *Dictionary of Symbols*, the pentagram, a five-pointed star, is such a symbol.[7] The five points are a stylized representation of a person with arms outstretched. This ideogram represents both primordial and generic humanity. Said another way, the five-pointed star symbolizes human beings as miniature representations of the greater life pattern of the cosmos. The five senses and elements are represented by the pentagram. An apple sliced horizontally depicts five seeds in the shape of a pentagram. Not coincidentally, many cultures have selected the apple as the quintessence of knowledge; a well-known example is the story in Genesis. When Adam and Eve ate the apple, a cataclysmic change took place which required them to leave their garden of paradise and become self-conscious beings, subject to the dualities of good and evil. The Great Pyramid is a mathematical monument to the number five and, therefore, the pentagram. Pyramids incorporate both celestial and terrestrial measurements in their architecture and depict the mystery of life as well as the relationship between the temporal and the eternal.[8]

The following statements come from a wide variety of spiritual traditions, yet have a common underlying theme. The diversity of the cultures and historical periods from which these statements are derived lends credence to the notion that The Principle of Correspondence can be a relevant and meaningful part of our lives.[9]

> The without is like the within of things, the small is like the large.
>
> ... HERMES TRISMEGISTUS

> What is here is elsewhere.
>
> ... HINDU VISVASARA TANTRA

> The macrocosm is the microcosm.
>
> ... TWELFTH-CENTURY SUFI SAYING

> Anywhere is the center of the world.
>
> ... BLACK ELK (Sioux medicine man)

God is a circle whose center is everywhere, and its circumference nowhere.

... EMPEDOCLES (Greek philosopher)

... each object in the world is not merely itself, but involves every other object and, in fact, is everything else.

... HINDU AVATAMSAKA SUTRA

What these ancient statements and The Principle of Correspondence portray is identical with the holographic model of the universe mentioned previously. Physicist David Bohm believes that everything in the cosmos is made of a seamless holographic fabric. Just as every portion of a hologram contains the image of the whole, every portion of the universe includes the whole. Every cell in our body enfolds the entire cosmos as does every flower, every speck of sand and every raindrop. Separating reality into parts and naming those parts help us, on one level, to analyze and understand the universe. If carried too far, it can mislead us. Subatomic particles, like everything else in existence, are no more separate from one another than are different patterns in an ornate tapestry. It can be argued, therefore, that our tendency to fragment the world and ignore the intimate connection is responsible for many of our problems: in the field of science, in our personal and business relationships or in our religious and cultural interactions.[10]

While many people give lip service to the idea that we are all one, it seems much harder to practice, particularly on an unconditional, no-exceptions basis. We all have problems relating to some of our friends or acquaintances, and we probably all know someone whose behavior or attitude is anathema, certainly not worthy of a supporting or loving relationship. Rabbi Shmelke, a Hasidic master, answers this very problem for a disciple:

A disciple asked Rabbi Shmelke: "We are commanded to love our neighbor as ourself. How can I do this, if my neighbor has wronged me?"

The rabbi answered: "You must understand these words aright. Love your neighbor like something which you yourself are. For all souls are one. Each is a spark from the original soul, and this soul is wholly inherent in all souls, just as your soul is in all the members of your body. It may come to pass that your hand makes a mistake and strikes you. But would you then take a stick and chastise your hand, because it lacked understanding, and so increase your pain? It is the same if your neighbor, who is of one soul with you, wrongs you for lack of understanding. If you punish him, you only hurt yourself."

The disciple went on asking: "But if I see a man who is wicked before God, how can I love him?"

"Don't you know," said Rabbi Shmelke, "that the original soul came out of the essence of God, and that every human soul is a part of God? And will you have no mercy on him, when you see that one of his holy sparks has been lost in a maze, and is almost stifled?"[11]

The Rabbi is telling us that it is in our own interest to follow the golden rule. Someone else's problem eventually becomes our problem if the point of contention is not satisfactorily resolved. In addition, our supposed adversaries are often more helpful to us than our friends. In the *Tao Te Ching*, Lao Tzu puts an interesting spin on this idea, "What is a good man but a bad man's teacher? What is a bad man but a good man's job?"[12] Our "petty tyrants," a term used in Carlos Castaneda's books to symbolize our antagonists, give us just what we need; it is a wise person who is thankful for their presence.

On a physical level, if we disregard a pain in our body it will likely get worse until it gets our attention. In society at large, if we ignore the "have-nots," we are faced with crime, drugs and the rising costs of welfare. If we worry about pollution only on the beach we frequent, the fish we consume from the adjoining beach will soon become contaminated. Until enough conscious beings accept the holographic model that tells us we are all one, we all suffer the consequences.

DOING BUSINESS IN A HOLOGRAPHIC UNIVERSE

A business is, likewise, a holographic organism and, having moved beyond dualistic thinking where mind and matter are separate, we begin to recognize that seemingly isolated problems in the enterprise are often a reflection of the health of the whole organization. Where is the system not working? Where is it failing to provide an atmosphere that promotes a satisfied, productive work force? How many employees are affected and how much time and energy could be saved if the work environment and vision of the business were modified? By embracing a holistic model, leaders of a corporation can connect to the whole organization by focusing on a small slice of the work force. A representative group of employees can function as the decision-making team for the entire enterprise. In fact, holographic thinking encourages us to re-examine our perceptions about who the leaders of an organization really are. Empowering employees at all levels to take greater responsibility and exercise a greater amount of authority often raises the level of motivation, creativity and productivity throughout the organization.[13]

As cooperation takes precedence over competition when we move from separation to connection, so cocreation becomes a preeminent part of the work environment when the concept of being intimately united replaces that of being superficially connected. There are some blurred lines between cooperation and cocreation; in the former the boundaries are more rigid, while in the latter they are open, allowing a fusing or synergistic effect to take place. As we have mentioned previously, notwithstanding the fact that an organization is set up to function cocreatively, competition and cooperation remain. Cocreation may elicit a greater degree of innovation and enthusiasm, but it does require compromise and surrender on the part of the participants. It also requires that one be detached and freer of concern about the outcome. Finally, participants need to acknowledge that it is all right to need help from others. Thus some combination among these three modes of interaction—competition, cooperation and cocreation—is undoubtedly optimum. While start-up companies in general and creative firms in particular lend themselves to being organized cocreatively, larger enterprises are also moving in this direction.[14]

OPENING TO COCREATION

A business's prosperity is closely tied to its employees' productivity, creativity and motivation. To nurture an effective and satisfied work force, a growing number of companies over the past decade have adopted a new approach to communicating and interacting with employees. It is called "Open Book Management" (OBM) and involves teaching everyone on the payroll to understand, monitor and, most importantly, take responsibility for the company's financial performance. Companies engaged in this practice expect employees to think and act like owners rather than hired hands who simply put in eight hours and then go home. To engender an elevated level of commitment, open book management gives all workers access to pertinent company records and a large financial stake in the company's earnings. It brings the objectives of management and labor into harmonious alignment and is, therefore, an ideal structure to pursue cocreative activities.

Opening financial statements to all employees is not an easy step for management to take. It requires courage to make previously guarded information widely accessible and it lessens the employer's ability to control and dominate the workers. In a sense, all managers become workers and all workers become managers. Impetus for taking such a drastic step often comes as a result of a financial crisis. Short of bankruptcy, there are usually few options left. Such was the case with two of the most well known practitioners of open book management, Cin-Made Corporation, a manufacturer of composite cans and paper tubes, and SRC, an engine remanufacturing company.

Contrary to what might be thought, opening the books is not always greeted enthusiastically by employees. They must assume new responsibilities and duties; often set their own production schedules and take responsibility for purchasing materials and making hiring decisions. At SRC, for instance, machinists decided to put in more overtime rather than hire new people to fill two openings. Training new employees costs money—a significant portion of which goes to the employees under their open book agreement. The entire labor force now needs to understand financial statements, something that non-accountants can find difficult if not intimidating. In short, everyone has to begin to think like an owner. To be successful, a high degree of trust must be established among coworkers as it takes time to learn new skills and patience to realize the financial and psychological benefits.

Such a system can have a big payoff. The historic adversarial relationship between management and labor ceases, almost by definition. Absenteeism and turnover are likely to abate; morale will certainly rise. Added responsibilities challenge employees and they take greater pride in their work as they feel more essential and better appreciated. Last, but not least, the bottom line inevitably improves to the benefit of everyone. In the case of Cin-Made, the company went from being a financial catastrophe to being quite profitable. SRC transformed itself from a money losing organization to one capable of achieving pretax profits of 6 percent in an industry with millimeter-size margins.[15]

SATURN—A COCREATIVE "STAR"

In 1981, General Motors was experiencing the effects of a prolonged recession, severe foreign competition and combative labor relations. The company was losing money and had to lay off close to 170,000 union employees. To respond to this challenge, GM put together a team from various departments to determine if it would be technologically feasible to build a small car in the United States. The group was dubbed the Saturn Project. Using a "clean-sheet" approach not bound by traditional thinking and industry practices, GM and the United Auto Workers (UAW) both recognized the need to find new approaches to union-management relations. In total, ninety-nine GM and UAW people were brought together.[16] The guiding philosophy under which this team operated was articulated as follows:

> We believe that all people want to be involved in decisions that affect them, care about their jobs, take pride in themselves and in their contributions and want to share in the success of their effort. By creating an atmosphere of mutual trust and respect, recognizing and utilizing individual expertise and knowledge in innovative ways, providing the technologies and education for each individual, we will enjoy a successful relationship and a sense of belonging to an integrated business system capable of achieving our common goals which insures security for our people and success for our business and communities.[17]

On October 25, 1990, seven years after the Saturn project was publicly announced, the first vehicles became available at Saturn retailers. Saturn ranked as number one in new car sales per facility in 1991, marking the first time in fifteen years that a U.S. nameplate topped the list. On April 15, 1992, Saturn received Motor-Week/PBS television's "1992 Drivers' Choice Award for Best Small Car" for the second year in a row. In May 1993, Saturn reported its first monthly operating profit. In June 1994, 16 percent of all Saturn customers participated in "The Saturn Homecoming" at Spring Hill, Tennessee where they toured the plant, met the work force and socialized with other Saturn owners.[18] Since its first model year, Saturn has received consistently high scores from J.D. Power and Associates in a number of new car categories, achieving a record in the New Car Sales Satisfaction Index Study in 1995.[19] Saturn tied for first place with Toyota's luxury brand, Lexus, in J.D. Power's 1996 customer satisfaction survey.[20] And, in a May 1997 press release, Strategic Vision (SV), a San Diego-based research firm, reported that Saturn continued to dominate SV's Dealer Total Quality Award for brands under $20,000.[21]

What are the characteristics of Saturn's management-union partnership that enabled them to achieve these significant accomplishments? The key points are listed below:

- The focus is on long-term job security and not short-term economic gain.
- The needs of the people are balanced with technology and business systems.
- Workers must be provided the opportunity to gain dignity, self-fulfillment and a sense of worth.
- Productivity and quality are a means to improving standards of living and quality of life for all.
- Workers and their representatives practice in the management of the business.
- Decision making and authority are decentralized through the empowerment of workers.
- The voice of the worker is recognized as legitimate and meaningful at all levels of the decision making process without an opportunity for cooptation.
- A safe workplace is expected, required and provided.
- Pride and loyalty to corporation and product are evident.
- A reasonable return on investment is the goal.
- Conflict is managed constructively without being adversarial.[22]

A major part of the success of this innovative automobile company is attributable to the fact that, from the beginning, Saturn has operated in a cooperative and cocreative manner. A groundbreaking collective bargaining agreement now empowers workers at all levels. Compared to contracts with other GM employees, Saturn workers have much greater insight into the company's financial condition and greater control over day-to-day operations. Using a scaled down open book management arrangement, Saturn puts up to 10% of a worker's pay "at risk" conditioned upon meeting production performance objectives.[23]

The Saturn project was much more ambitious and broader in scope than General Motors' other cooperative efforts. GM's collaboration with Ford, Chrysler and several government agencies, as outlined in the previous chapter, has narrowly defined objectives with little likelihood of any large scale synergistic effects. With Saturn, however, as trust was built between management and labor, many side benefits accrued. The company's corridors are said to reverberate with discussions of alternative ways of doing the job. When asked about a "new idea" program, an employee responded, "New ideas are expected as a part of my job. No incentives are expected or need be given."[24] Furthermore, there is an informal understanding that every employee should be looking out for the customer. This involves everything from asking people on the street how they like their cars to making it their personal responsibility to sell their neighbors and relatives on the merits of their cars. Thus Saturn employees have become unpaid marketing agents for the company.

This sense of responsibility spills over to virtually every relationship the company forms, from the neighboring environment, to their retailers and customers. Even suppliers, whom companies often view as more foe than friend, play a cocreative role at Saturn. Titan Services, a firm that designs and manufactures one-of-a-kind tools and machinery, suggested early in the brainstorming discussions that they put their people directly on the factory floor. Today, half of Titan's staff works at Saturn's plant. According to Christy Hoffmann, an employee of Titan who works at Saturn, "This is much more than just a job to go to. It gets in your blood—your heart's involved. Those people, the team you work with, mean a lot to you. You'll go that extra mile for them."[25] Thus everyone connected with Saturn is made to feel a part of the team which functions under the same written philosophy: "We, the Saturn Team, in concert with the UAW and General Motors, believe that meeting the needs of Saturn's customers, suppliers, dealers, and neighbors is fundamental to fulfilling our mission."[26] Obviously, it all revolves around people. Speaking at Stanford University, Jack O'Toole, a Vice President of the UAW who was very involved with the Saturn project, made the following remarks:

> During the past seven years, we've become convinced the most technological piece of machinery a company can employ is the human. The model organization of the 21st century will be the one where the talents and potential of the entire workforce is fully utilized. . . . People need to embrace the proper attitude if they are to do a world-class job. It isn't enough just to show them what the process is and how to operate it—the company of the 21st century has to give them the desire to want to do a world-class job. The desire to excel has to come from **within** (emphasis added).[27]

WHAT IS WITHIN?

As may be recalled, in a state of separation we identify with our body. This is understandable given our reliance on the five senses to feed us and to alert us to potential predators. In one way or another almost every conscious moment was spent fighting for our physical survival. Then, as civilization evolved and day-to-day existence became less of an issue, we shifted our priorities to the gratification of the senses. We believe that if we can acquire and accumulate more things we will be happy and content. Under the law of diminishing returns, however, physical pleasures do not bring us the meaning and fulfillment we had expected; they are too transitory and shallow. When we reach the point where we realize that we are part of an infinite, eternal, living organism, both survival and sense gratification recede in importance and a longing for deeper understanding and meaning begins to take precedence. Instead of directing our attention almost solely toward the body, we begin to look beyond the physical vehicle to what remains after the body disintegrates and the personality "dies."

The name given this eternal "center of expression" varies from culture to culture; in the West it is usually referred to as the soul. It is the enduring essence or divine spark that resides in all of life. It is forever striving for harmony with the laws of the universe; it makes no judgments, has no fears and exists outside of the boundaries of space and time. It has reverence for all of life and, as we align ourselves with it, we attract all that is needed. The literal meaning of the Hindu word "yoga" is union, most specifically, with our eternal essence. We are told that attaining this union eliminates pain and confusion replacing them with inner resilience, contentment and security. Even life's problems become a joyful challenge as tackling them gives us a sense of resourcefulness, strength and creative ability.[28] Perhaps most importantly, as we experience the intimate connection to the source of life, the certain knowledge of our proper place in the universe is revealed.

DOWNSHIFTING TO SMOOTH THE RIDE

How do we get to the point where we want to reverse our priorities from a preoccupation with external, physical stimuli to a state where we become drawn toward internal, spiritual endeavors? The perennial philosophy of all sacred traditions tells us, in a variety of ways, to "know thyself." A number of statements that make this point have previously been cited from a variety of religious writings. Being observant and mindful of all our thoughts and actions enables us to expand our consciousness through self-discovery. There is no better environment for gaining self-knowledge than the one in which we earn our livelihood; it gives us limitless opportunities to see what motivates us, frightens us, angers us and enlivens us. In today's Western culture, the linchpin for business and economics is money. To quote philosopher Jacob Needleman:

> Money in the modern era is a purely secular force, reflecting the lower nature of man. Cut off from any relation to spiritual aspiration, it has become the most obvious example of a fire raging out of control. Our challenge is to bring money back to the place where it belongs in human life. . . . And that place is *secondary*. Our aim is to understand what it means to make money secondary in life. As a principal representative of the lower nature,

the outward, physical body of man, money must become secondary, as the body must become secondary. . . . And if money
is to be secondary in our lives, it can only mean that money serve
the aim of self-knowledge.[29]

This means that money should be used as a tool for studying ourselves as we are and as we can become. By doing so we
learn to discriminate between those things that are truly needed
and for the highest good, and those that keep us chained to satisfying our senses and living in a state of fear and disease. Once
our discernment matures to the point that we know that more
goods and services are not bringing us what we want, we are
compelled to look elsewhere. Gradually we turn inward where
we find unlimited opportunities for expanding our awareness
and understanding who we are and what we are doing here.
These experiences are not subject to diminishing returns; they
are liberating and fulfilling.

An increasing number of people are beginning to find themselves at this crossroad. Images of Hermes, god of the roads and
protector of travelers, have long topped pillars as guideposts
along roadways and at critical junctures everywhere. Hermes'
steadfast guidance, for those at a turning point, is to seek balance;
find the middle term or path in all things.[30] Such counsel is well
worth heeding whether the subject concerns the sacred or the
profane. And lately many of the spiritual aspects of life are coming to the forefront. A cover article in *Newsweek*, entitled "The
Search for the Sacred: America's Quest for Spiritual Meaning," reported significant evidence that there is a deep yearning for a sacred dimension in life. Fifty-eight percent of those polled by the
magazine said they feel the need to experience spiritual growth.
A third of all adults reported having had a mystical or religious
experience. The magazine attributed this hunger for meaning to a
variety of cultural phenomena ranging from baby boomers reaching the contemplative phase of life to a general dissatisfaction
with the materialism of the modern world. Americans seem to be
searching for harmony with the cosmic order and a sense of com-
munion with its source, according to the article.[31]

Echoing and updating these findings is research conducted by Gerald Celente, director of the Trends Research Institute in Rhinebeck, New York. More and more people are trying to zero in on the issues that are really important in their lives. As part of this spiritual renaissance Celente's studies found that about four million baby boomers have begun to embrace voluntary simplicity by concentrating more on the quality of their lives than on the accumulation of possessions.[32] Some of the most common changes include reducing work hours, changing to a lower-paying job and quitting work to stay at home. The vast majority of those who have made the change claim to be happy with their decisions and, in contrast to the population as a whole, are happier than their parents were at the same age. A Los Angeles woman described her decision to "downshift" her priorities as follows:

> As I started climbing the corporate ladder, I really decided that I was hating it more and more, and I was bringing more and more work home. . . . I was already hiring people to clean my clothes, watch my kid, and now clean my house. And I changed careers and got paid less. I sold the car and I bought a '65 Ford Falcon. . . . And I'm much happier. I work two blocks from home and I'm doing something I really enjoy.[33]

Several decades of watching how I, as well as scores of my clients, react to fluctuations in the value of financial assets has convinced me that there is little correlation between the amount of money people have and their sense of happiness or fulfillment. Some clients lead a carefree meaningful life on relatively modest incomes; others have much more and never feel it is enough. Likewise, those who have inherited enough money to provide a multitude of material comforts are often in a constant state of turmoil and discontent. Often, finding that material goods are not providing the peace and contentment we desire, we begin to look elsewhere.

These new "downshifters," by reorienting their lives from an almost exclusive concentration on outer-directed activities to a more balanced weighting of inner and outer-directed efforts, are following Hermes' advice and finding life much more satisfying. This transformation will have profound effects on all aspects of life, but none any more dramatic than on the world of business. According to Gary Zukav, author of the internationally acclaimed best-seller *The Dancing Wu Li Masters:*

> As individuals within the business community come to recognize themselves as immortal souls, and experience within themselves the shift from pursuit of external power— the ability to manipulate and control—to pursuit of authentic power—alignment of the personality with the soul . . . all relationships between businesses will be defined by the ability of each enterprise to contribute to Life, and to assist other enterprises to contribute to Life. Negotiations will center not over extending control, but over providing resources. Conferences will be held not to exploit the weaknesses of competitors, but to augment the strengths of friends. Assessments will be made to determine which enterprise is most able to provide the need of society that is under consideration, and how it can best be supported by others.[34]

A transformation of major proportions, predicted by sages and prophets and delivered in an assortment of communications, is at hand. Although many remain skeptical, those who adjust their behavior to harmonize with the new realities are likely to reap the benefits. The Principle of Cause and Effect is at work at all times and in all places.

LOOKING BACK

Let us review what has been covered. We evolve from a state of isolation, in which many painful mistakes are made, to a stage where we awaken to some of life's interconnections and then to a point of seeing the unity of all that exists. These three stages, with some of the diverse terminology used for describing this progression, are summarized in Table 5–1.

Table 5–1 Humanity and Business—Evolving Together

STAGE ONE	STAGE TWO	STAGE THREE
Competition	Cooperation	Cocreation
Separate	Connected	United
M-1	M-2	M-3
Self-Love	Social Awareness	Global Responsibility
Body	Body/Mind	Soul

In the process of evolving humans learn from their self-created problems and consequently recognize that they are eternal souls, not temporal bodies. The most satisfying goal then becomes more conscious awareness rather than more physical gratification. We see ourselves as a small but essential part of a living organism, and realize that we can understand our place in the macrocosm through The Principle of Correspondence. By studying the part we can know the whole just as scrutinizing a cell gives us information about our entire body.

LOOKING AHEAD—CONSCIOUSLY

Since the fall of communism in the late 1980s, various renditions of the free enterprise system have been put in place in countries around the globe. Most people know that capitalism is a market based economic system where the means of production and distribution are privately owned and controlled. It is the system that seems best able to reflect the free flowing, multidimensional nature of life and is, therefore, capable of facilitating responsible, flexible and expeditious solutions to the problems of a dynamic, growing economy. What many fail to realize is that capitalism can have a number of configurations ranging from cutthroat competition, through selective cooperation, to cocreative partnering. Depending on circumstances, some combination of these three modes of operation will maximize economic prosperity. Conscious capitalism, reflecting the higher aspects of human nature and honoring the interdependence of life, is based on the understanding that harmonious relationships are essential to everyone's sense of fulfillment and well-being. As such, cocreation and cooperation necessarily play a preeminent role. As documented more thoroughly in the next few chapters, companies that practice conscious capitalism not only "do good" for society but "do well" for all their constituencies. Most importantly, and perhaps paradoxically, the major beneficiaries of conscious capitalism are business shareholders and/or owners. Let us see why this is so.

NOTES

1. Harman, p. 34.

2. Plato. *The Dialogues*, Vol. IV, Laws X, trans. B. Jowett, 4th ed. (Oxford: Clarendon Press, 1964), p. 474.

3. Capra, p. 29.

4. Rosemary Ellen Guiley. *The Encyclopedia of Dreams: Symbols and Interpretations* (New York: Berkley Books, 1995), p. xii.

5. Breton and Largent, pp. 130–133.

6. *The One and the Many*, p. 11.

7. Carl G. Liungman. *Dictionary of Symbols* (Santa Barbara, CA: ABC-CLIO, 1991), p. 44.

8. Dusty Bunker. *Quintiles and Tredeciles: The Geometry of the Goddess* (West Chester, PA: Whitford Press, a division of Schiffer Publishing, Ltd, 1989), pp. 27–28.

9. Michael Talbot. *The Holographic Universe* (New York: HarperCollins, 1991), pp. 290–292.

10. Ibid, pp. 48–49.

11. Martin Buber, ed., *Tales of the Hasidim*, rev. ed. in 1 vol. (New York: Schocken Books, 1975), p. 190.

12. Novak, p. 147.

13. Carol Sanford. "A Self-Organizing Leadership View of Paradigms," in *New Traditions in Business: Spirit and Leadership in the 21st Century*, ed. John Renesch (San Francisco: Berrett-Koehler Publishers, 1992), pp. 204–205.

14. Joba, Maynard, Jr. and Ray, pp. 50–56.

15. Jaclyn Fierman. "Winning Ideas from Maverick Managers," *Fortune*, 6 February 1995, p. 68.

16. Jack O'Toole and Jim Lewandowski. "Forming the Future: The Marriage of People and Technology at Saturn," Presented to Stanford University Industrial Engineering and Engineering Management (Palo Alto, CA: 29 March 1990), reproduced by Saturn Corporation, Spring Hill, TN, p. 2.

17. Ibid, p. 3.

18. *Important Dates in Saturn History* (Spring Hill, TN: Saturn Corporation, 1995), pp. 2–9.

19. "JD Power Initial Quality Rankings," *USA Today*, 8 May 1996, p. 2(B).

20. "Saturn, Lexus Customers Found to Be Most Satisfied in Survey," *Investor's Business Daily*, 14 June 1996, p. 15(B).

21. "When It Comes to Service, General Motors Tops All," *Investor's Business Daily*, 28 May 1997, p. 2(A).

22. Michael E. Bennett. "The Saturn Corporation: New Management-Union Partnership at the Factory of the Future," *Looking Ahead*, XIII, 4 (April 1992): p. 23, reproduced by Saturn Corporation, Spring Hill, TN.

23. Paul A. Eisenstein. "GM Saturn's Hudler: On Treating People Right from Shop Floor to Showroom," *Investor's Business Daily*, 20 December 1996, p. 1(A).

24. *Saturn Catalogue* (Spring Hill, TN: Saturn Corporation, 1994), p. 4.

25. Ibid, pp. 4–9.

26. Richard G. LeFauve. "The Saturn Corporation: A Balance of People, Technology and Business Systems," *Looking Ahead*, XIII, 4 (April, 1992): p. 16, reproduced by Saturn Corporation, Spring Hill, TN.

27. O'Toole, p. 3.

28. Eva Pierrakos. *The Pathwork of Self-Transformation*, comp. & ed. Judith Saly (New York: Bantam Books, 1990), pp. 4–5.

29. Needleman, pp. 70–72.

30. *Compton's Interactive Encyclopedia* 1996 ed., s.v. "Hermes" [CD-ROM] (Compton's NewMedia, 1995).

31. Barbara Kantrowitz. "Search for the Sacred," *Newsweek*, 28 November 1994, p. 53.

32. Joanne Cleaver. "The Spirit of Success," *Home Office Computing*, May 1996, p. 104.

33. *Yearning for Balance*, prepared for the Merck Family Fund by The Harwood Group, July 1995, p. 18.

34. Gary Zukav. "Evolution and Business," in *The New Paradigm in Business: Emerging Strategies for Leadership and Organizational Change*, ed. Michael Ray and Alan Rinzler (New York: Putnam Publishing Group for the World Business Academy, 1993), p. 245.

6

Top Line, Bottom Line, "Inner Line"

What does business have to do with the inner life (line) of its employees or the evolution of the planet's consciousness? The sole responsibility of business, many will argue, is to earn the highest possible profit for its owners. They put up the *capital* resources and took the risks. But to look only at how increasing revenues or cutting expenses improves the bottom line misses the other two parts of the resource equation. *Human* resources (employees, customers and suppliers) and *natural* resources (land and what lives on and around it) are also of critical importance. In this chapter we will look at the role of business from an all encompassing, long-term perspective thereby connecting what is sown with what is reaped.

H. B. Fuller Company, a billion dollar manufacturer of specialty chemicals, has increased earnings approximately eighteen-fold since its founding in 1968; equal to a double digit compound annual rate of growth. This is an outstanding record of achievement.[1] The last two sentences of its three-sentence mission statement read as follows:

> H. B. Fuller Company is committed to its responsibilities, *in order of priority*, [emphasis added] to its customers, employees, shareholders and communities. H. B. Fuller will conduct business legally and ethically, support the activities of its employees in their communities and be a responsible corporate citizen.[2]

One must have capital to start a business, but capital can derive no return in the absence of satisfied customers and productive employees. Furthermore, all the money in the world will be of little comfort if the community in which one lives is dirty, dangerous and/or lacking in opportunity for its citizens. More specifically, rising crime rates cost businesses billions of dollars every year; a poorly educated work force compromises a corporation's ability to compete in an increasingly high-tech world; a polluted biosphere increases health, legal and insurance costs; unappreciated employees will constantly be looking for a different employer. Regarding turnover, it is estimated to cost up to 75 percent of a year's salary to replace an hourly employee and 150 percent of a year's salary to replace a manager.[3] Only very shortsighted speculators would conclude that solutions to personnel and community problems are not in their self-interest. An investor in the true sense of the word takes the long-term view that, unless societal problems are solved, business will suffer. According to Jim Autry, retired president of the magazine group of Meredith Corporation, a Fortune 500 company:

> I'm against those who say a corporation's only social responsibility is to its stockholders . . . business is simply one part of a large and complicated ecosystem, which includes government, education, health care, really the entire social order. For corporations to say our only responsibility is to stockholders is to deny our place in the ecosystem.[4]

It is clearly in business' interest to pay as much attention to the "inner line" as the bottom line. Moreover, the business world is the sector of society best equipped to assume this very important role. Larry Perlman, CEO of Ceridian Corporation, a multibillion dollar information services business, believes:

For better or worse, work is where most of us find our sense of meaning. I see a huge opportunity to participate in the transformation of this country, and to do so we must transform business.[5]

Meryem LeSaget, founder of Erasme International, a French communications and consulting firm, shares these sentiments:

The business community will be the most coherent over the next dozen or so years, which means it's where the real changes will take place. Business has the knowledge, the money, the networks, and the technology to lead society into a new future.[6]

Competitive necessity requires businesses to respond quickly to changing market forces. Our religious institutions, governments and learning organizations have become too cumbersome and politicized for today's fast pace. The modern business enterprise is society's most adaptive institution. Corporations cross national boundaries with as much frequency and, in many cases, with more skill than our political institutions. Unfortunately, they are often overregulated by these same inefficient and bureaucratic agencies. Faced with deciding between onerous regulations from government or the responsibility of self-regulating for society's benefit, a company's choice should be obvious.

As discussed in the last chapter, everything is not only connected but intimately united. Life is a holistic phenomenon, each person a living organism in a living universe. Just as each body is a collection of cells working together for the good of the whole; each cell is a miniature body carrying on all functions of the body including ingestion, digestion, waste removal and reproduction. The well-being of the body is dependent upon the good health of each and every one of its cells.[7] By analogy, a business, which is, in reality, a living organization composed of living bodies (employees), must create a healthy, vibrant environment for all its parts if it is to achieve its goals. When business looks at its responsibilities to society from the perspective of a living system, it

finds that pressure to change its structure and priorities is building from four directions: the inside out, the bottom up, the outside in and the top down.

INSIDE OUT

Just as every atom of our being places demands on the rest of the
body, all levels of an organization exert claims on its resources;
both are alive and need to be nurtured. This living organization
model has been put to the test on some of Bristol-Myers Squibb
Company's production lines. As described in a report to shareholders:

> For the most part, mass production always has demanded
> increasing specialization, with workers separated into quasi-
> autonomous groups like machinists, maintenance people and
> engineers. These days, though, employees at many Bristol-Myers
> plants are returning to a simpler, more natural work style built
> around units called cells. Each work cell includes people with
> different skills who join together to accomplish a task—such as
> making artificial hips. And each cell has considerable autonomy
> in setting its own schedule and assignments to meet customer
> demand.[8]

Work cells not only promote efficiency but, to quote one of
the team members, "We all feel a greater pride of ownership in
the products we create." As a result, the time required to change
the line from one product to another has been reduced from forty
minutes to ten minutes. Workers change duties every two months;
boredom is minimized and there is a greater sense of being an essential part of the end product.[9] Reverting to a more natural way
to work—a living organism within a living organization—enhances worker productivity and self-esteem and everyone in the
organization benefits. That which is within, the cells of a body or
the bodies of an organization, continually pressure the larger entity to provide an environment conducive to health and happi-

ness. The business that fails to heed internal signs of disease will, at best, operate below its potential.

BOTTOM UP

Living organisms rely on two systems for learning and adapting—a central nervous system that distributes information about current events and DNA that provides instructions on how to react to those events. Some of today's most successful corporations have created "corporate nervous systems" to supply critical information not only from the top down but, in the case of the farsighted ones, from the bottom up.[10] Even if the concept of business as a living organization is rejected, the more traditional hierarchical structure will also come to recognize many of the same demands for change. The needs and desires of today's workforce differ dramatically from those of a short time ago. As Dr. P. Roy Vagelos, former chairman and chief executive officer of Merck, stated:

> A company's success is largely dependent on its ability to adapt to change in many areas. Much change has taken place in the lifestyles of our work force as evidenced by the growing number of working women, dual-career couples, single parents and women with young children. Responsiveness to the needs of this changed population, we feel, is key in our ability to attract and keep good people.[11]

As a case in point, a Merck unit in Canada decided to assess employees' work-family conflicts. A focus group with two hundred employees revealed some of the problems. Salespeople, who increasingly used computers to record sales data, were being hounded by their managers for more analytical reports. Some were spending nights and weekends crunching numbers. Others were staying at home during the day to do the reports, then feeling guilty about it. This affected not only sales but morale in general. Merck formed a task force of managers to study the focus group feedback. The managers confirmed that many of the reports were not required and cut the number by more than half. The result was salespeople gaining extra time each week to see customers and pursue personal interests including their often neglected and resentful families. According to Merck's Perry Christensen, the initiative came from the employees themselves. Their work-family desires were the driving force that compelled the company to focus in on which work was most important.[12]

By the mid-1990s women held 46 percent of total jobs versus 35 percent 30 years earlier. For the most part they have started at the bottom and worked for less. Nonetheless, they are exerting an increasing influence on corporations worldwide. In a few years, the majority of net new entrants into the workforce will be women. Perhaps three-quarters of them will become pregnant at some point in their careers; most will return to work before their child's first birthday. As our population ages a growing percentage of workers, primarily women, will need time and resources to care for their parents.[13]

A study entitled *Women: The New Providers* looked at the important and relevant family, work and social issues facing women in the United States. Some of the conclusions of the study were what might have been expected; more flexible hours, more opportunities to work at home and more part-time work were all high priorities. Both men and women expressed an extraordinary level of interest in less than full-time work so they could better juggle their wage-earning and care-giving responsibilities. According to the study, women seem to exhibit commitment, internal motivation, a concern for quality, a desire for lifelong learning and a flexible, independent approach to work. These are all characteristics that are considered essential for the workplace of the future. Management that ignores the needs or desires of these "New Providers" is going to have a difficult time retaining these employees; the resulting high turnover and poor morale could be serious negative influences on the bottom line.[14]

OUTSIDE IN

Compared to the pressure generated by a company's workforce, the demands for change coming from pressure groups outside the organization may be even more compelling. The chance of successfully convincing a corporation to take social as well as economic issues into account is increased when the target is a company in which one is a stockholder. The greater the size of the stock holding, the better the chance of gaining management's attention. As far back as the early 1970s, Princeton University was pressured by its student body to add moral and social criteria to the usual economic ones in making decisions regarding its endowment portfolio. Specifically, a group of students demanded that the university sell its holdings in firms with subsidiaries or affiliates operating in South Africa. At the time this amounted to $127 million or approximately one-third of the total portfolio. While the committee voted against selling their shares, they began to speak out forcefully against corporate practices they considered irresponsible. The president of Princeton sent a letter to corporations whose shares it held explaining the views of the committee and specifically urging the corporations to improve working conditions for black workers. While it is difficult to say how much effect Princeton had, those involved felt that continued pressure from large stockholders can change a company's policies.[15]

Investors with far less money than large institutions can encourage companies to do the right thing by placing their capital in mutual funds that invest in "socially responsible" businesses. A report issued at the end of 1997 by the nonprofit Social Investment Forum estimated that over $1 trillion under professional management is involved in some type of socially responsible investing (SRI). This is up from $65 billion in 1985 and represents almost one-tenth of the total funds under professional management in the United States.[16] While the records of these funds vary widely, the underlying premise is that businesses which treat their employees well, do not sell harmful products, protect the environment and give back to the community should be successful in the long term. In fact, a study conducted by researchers at Vanderbilt University and the Investor Responsibility Research Center found that "cleaner" corporations perform as well or better than "dirtier" firms in the same industry categories.[17]

Recognizing that a larger audience could be attracted to the SRI concept if investors knew what, if any, financial sacrifice might be required, the investment firm of Kinder, Lydenberg, Domini Co., Inc. (KLD) constructed the Domini Social Index (DSI). It provides a quantitative benchmark against which socially responsible investments can be measured. On May 1, 1990, after twenty-six months of screening and analysis, four hundred diversified, large-capitalization stocks that passed a series of representative SRI filters and appraisals were selected and became the basis for their index. The DSI 400, contrary to the expectations of those who thought restrictions would necessarily hinder results, has outperformed the comparable indices cumulatively and over most annual intervals. An SRI index fund, the Domini Social Equity Fund, has had a similar record, closely mirroring the performance of the S&P 500. Considering the fact that the majority of professional investors have underperformed the popular averages in recent years, this record is impressive and reinforces the notion that investors can make a social statement without penalizing their wallets. Just as importantly, SRI sends a message of encouragement to those companies already following holistic business practices and goads those not yet on board.[18]

Socially responsible investing is by no means a strictly American phenomenon. Ethically managed funds in the UK have attracted over £1 billion. A recent survey found 95% of the adult population in Britain agrees with the statement, "I want my investment to benefit companies which are helping rather than harming the world." Friends Provident Stewardship Trust was launched in 1984; since then it has quadrupled in value and outperformed seventy-five of the top one hundred equity growth unit trusts in the UK. Ethical Investment Research Services (EIRIS) is an overseas watchdog group that monitors portfolios to ensure that managers adhere to their self-imposed ethical standards. In the UK, this generally means avoiding companies involved in arms sales, environmental pollution, countries with oppressive regimes, nuclear power, cruelty to animals, alcohol, tobacco, gambling or pornography. EIRIS has found that while investment performance is a top priority for only 41% of investors in SRI funds, a trust must deliver returns to attract new capital.[19] Although the Continent is behind Britain in the amount of money allocated to ethical investing, The European Union's tough social and environmental legislation is creating an atmosphere that will encourage attention to SRI issues.

An activist approach, which seems to get a fast response, is that taken by the California Public Employees' Retirement System (CalPERS). One of America's largest public pension funds with over $100 billion in assets, CalPERS commands attention. It sent a letter to two hundred chief executives asking them to lift the corporate veil on boardroom practices. Too often when company policies cross the ethical or legal line, the outside board members are unaware of the disdained practices. CalPERS wanted to know about the company's governance practices and, when not all companies answered promptly, CalPERS let the laggards know that the survey results would be made public. The responses rolled in; the information obtained will be used by CalPERS to determine which companies to target in the future.[20] A study by Gordon Group, a Newton, Massachusetts consulting firm found that a correlation exists between corporate results and "workplace performance." Based on this study, CalPERS took another controversial stance by announcing that it will consider how well companies respect the needs of their employees in making investment decisions. CalPERS wants to know, for example, whether companies offer employees training programs and give more responsibility to lower-level workers.[21] Commenting on CalPERS initiative, former Labor Secretary Robert Reich pointed out:

> This is really the first time that a major institutional investor has explicitly pointed to employer practices as important to its analysis of company performance. This "signal" by an institutional investor will have a far more dramatic impact than anything the Labor Department can say or do.[22]

A number of organizations have begun zeroing in on businesses' environmental practices. The International Organization for Standardization, based in Zurich, Switzerland was founded in 1946 to bring about worldwide standards for goods and services. It is best known for ISO 9000, which sets product-quality standards. Of growing importance, however, is ISO 14000 which establishes a long list of stringent rules to assure corporate environmental responsibility. There is likely to be considerable pressure on firms to adopt these standards as consumers, companies and governments request that their suppliers be ISO 14000 certified. Some one hundred countries have said they will support the standards which include the following requirements:

- Have an extensive, formal system for managing environmental affairs.
- Audit those systems based on specific criteria to ensure credibility.
- Set definitive bench marks for assessing environmental performance.
- Scrutinize the claims companies make about the environmental impact of their goods or services.

The standards require companies to aim for continual improvement in their environmental performance. According to Arthur B. Weissman, vice president of standards and planning for Green Seal, a group that certifies environmental claims made by corporations, ISO will eventually bring uniformity to the labeling process and give it credibility. He also believes it will save companies money by eliminating labeling certification fees now paid to a host of different organizations. In addition, ISO 14000 is likely to improve equity in international trade as businesses throughout the world will have to meet the same antipollution standards that many now disregard.[23]

There are dozens of other organizations from public service groups to trade confederations that are involved in assisting business in setting environmental standards and occasionally trying to "police" those standards. One that will be covered in some detail later in the book is CERES, the Coalition for Environmentally Responsible Economies. An organization that is a strong supporter and close ally of CERES is Co-op America. This nonprofit organization was founded in 1982 and has approximately forty-seven thousand individual members and nineteen hundred business members. Their programs and publications are simultaneously directed at the consumer (demand) and the business (supply) sides of the economy. Co-op America's agenda is focused on three primary objectives:

- Educate people on how to use their spending and investing dollars to foster greater social justice and environmental responsibility throughout the economy.
- Help environmentally and socially responsible businesses grow and prosper.
- Pressure irresponsible companies to accept environmentally and socially responsible practices.

Through its *National Green Pages* publication, Co-op America connects members and readers to the businesses of the Co-op America Business Network (CABN)—the largest association of green businesses in the world. All the business members of CABN sign The Green Business Ethics Pledge which states:

> As a member of the Co-op America Business Network, my company conducts business according to standards that reach beyond contemporary practices in addressing the needs of consumers, employees, the community and the environment.

I certify and can demonstrate that we strive to operate in a socially just and environmentally sustainable manner.[24]

The Natural Step (TNS) is an international organization, established in Sweden in 1989 to educate and train a wide variety of groups about the links between the ecology and the economy. TNS is based on the following four principles:

- Substances from the Earth's crust must not systematically increase in the biosphere. This implies that fossil fuels, metals and other minerals must not be extracted at a faster rate than their redeposit and reintegration into the Earth's crust.
- Substances produced by society must not systematically increase in nature. In other words, substances must not be produced faster than they can be broken down and reintegrated into natural cycles.
- The physical basis for the productivity and diversity of nature must not be systematically deteriorated. For example, don't harvest trees faster than they can be replenished.
- There needs to be fair and efficient use of resources with respect to meeting human needs.[25]

The Natural Step framework has been implemented in many countries and is being used by more than 60 corporations, including such industry leaders as Electrolux, Ikea and Interface. Interface, a carpet company with $800 million in annual sales, became, in June 1996, the first U.S. company to commit itself to the four TNS system conditions. With growing worldwide support from the scientific community and offices around the globe, TNS's influence in the business community is likely to increase in the years ahead.[26]

Business for Social Responsibility (BSR) is an organization with a more mainstream philosophy and clientele. They provide information, education, technical support and a variety of practical tools to member companies to help them implement responsible business practices. Founded in 1992, BSR has more than

1200 members and affiliates, including such well-known companies as Arthur Andersen, Bristol-Myers Squibb, Fannie Mae,
Hasbro, Home Depot, Reebok, Starbucks Coffee, Time-Warner,
and Viacom. Smaller companies represent a significant portion
of BSR's membership and have been given meaningful representation on its Board of Directors. About a third of the multi-
million dollar budget comes from dues; the rest from contributions
and grants from organizations such as Heinz Foundation, John
F. Merck Fund, Pew Charitable Trust, Ford Foundation, U.S. Department of Energy and EPA.[27]

The organizations described in this section have already
had a significant impact on the business community throughout
the world. As humanity increasingly accepts the interdependence
of all that exists, the influence of these organizations will be
greatly expanded.

TOP DOWN

The most obvious and effective means for instituting workplace
and environmental responsibility is for the President or Chief
Executive Officer of a business to believe in and champion the effort. This means not only determining the values the company is
to follow, but making sure someone is in charge of coordinating
the policies and seeing that they are observed from the top to the
bottom of the organization. To make a meaningful contribution,
policies must become an automatic and sustainable part of the
company's culture.

Levi Strauss is one of the best known companies to have
embraced a corporate wide, value-based philosophy. Its "Aspi-
ration Statement" was crafted by top management, not the human
resources department, and encompasses everything from diversity issues to ethical management practices. One-third of an employee's evaluation is based on "aspirational" behavior. According
to Chief Executive Robert D. Haas, "We are doing this because
we believe in the interconnection between liberating the talents of
our people and business success."[28]

Since 1984, when Haas became CEO, Levi Strauss has doubled the percentage of minority managers and women in management ranks has climbed over 50 percent. Both of these statistics are superior to those of the average United States corporation. Most of the plants are nonunion yet labor leaders give the company credit for maintaining some of the safest, most worker-friendly factories in the industry. And in what may be the richest and most unusual employee incentive plan ever implemented, CEO Haas announced in June 1996 that the company would reward its employees with bonuses averaging about a year's pay if management's predetermined, six-year performance goals are met. This impacts all 37,500 workers in sixty countries and is in sharp contrast to the actions of many other corporations which have retained the profits from productivity increases for the exclusive benefit of management and shareholders. Frank Nicholas, a vice president of the Union of Needletrades, Industrial and Textile Employees said, "We were flabbergasted when the company came around and said they wanted to share the wealth."[29]

Tom's of Maine is another company whose visionary founders, Tom and Kate Chappell, have been outspoken in their belief that a company is about more than profits. The company's mission statement takes into account the workplace, the marketplace and the global community. Each year it donates 10 percent of pretax profits to a variety of nonprofit organizations and encourages employees to take some time off, at company expense, to do volunteer work. Recycled materials are emphasized and when it comes to packaging "less is more." People from every part of the company are invited to participate in answering telephone calls from customers. This means employees have to learn about parts of the company with which they are otherwise unfamiliar and become conversant with customers' concerns and complaints. As the country's leading producer of natural personal-care products, Tom's of Maine has been built on a vision that combines the pursuit of profit with the good of the community, the environment and one another.[30]

While strong leadership at Levi Strauss and Tom's of Maine has been instrumental in developing organizations that are both profitable and socially responsible, it must be noted that both of these companies are privately owned. Neither has to be concerned with the pressures that arise when Wall Street is closely watching every detail of each quarterly earnings report. Neither are they subject to external criticism if they fail to deliver on some promises or expectations. It is much harder to have a long-term perspective or to take risks under the scrutiny of a horde of security analysts who are only concerned with short-term earnings projections and tomorrow's stock price movements. Two examples, one personal and one public, illustrate why investment professionals have become so fixated on short-term results.

The Not-So-Nifty Fifty

I began my investment career working for a bank in its research department. After three years, I was given responsibility for managing six common trust funds (mutual funds for trust accounts) whose aggregate market value was $200 million (in the early 70s that was real money). I felt proud and somewhat overwhelmed that I was given so much responsibility while still in my late twenties. The smallest of these funds, worth less than ten million dollars, had capital growth as its investment objective. When I took over management of the assets, in late 1971, a group of about fifty stocks, often referred to as the "nifty fifty," were very much in vogue. They included well-known, high-quality companies whose earnings were increasing at an above-average rate. IBM, Digital Equipment, Polaroid, and Kmart were a few of the companies in this select group. They had become so popular that they were selling at prices that were forty to fifty times the value of their current year's earnings. This is several times greater than the earnings multiple at which the market had traditionally been valued. Many on Wall Street considered them "one decision" stocks; just buy them—they'll never have to be sold. Because of this mentality, the prices of these stocks had reached what were, arguably, irrationally high levels. Being a contrarian at heart, I could not bring myself to participate in this mania. In most other respects, these stocks would have been appropriate investments for this fund; however, I thought the prices were exorbitantly inflated. Nevertheless, they continued to climb higher, reaching a peak in 1973. Because the growth fund I was managing was largely devoid of these "core holdings," it underperformed the popular indices in 1972.

Early in 1973, I was summoned to the office of the President of the bank. He told me that he was reassigning the growth fund I was managing to another person, since the performance of this fund was below what other growth funds had achieved. I pointed out that I had only been managing the portfolio for slightly over one year and I was confident there would be an opportunity to purchase these stocks at more favorable prices in the future. Needless to say I did not prevail. I felt humiliated at having failed, angry that I was not given more time to prove myself, and victimized by an irrational investment climate. I did gain some measure of vindication when the market in general and these "one decision" stocks in particular lost a great deal of their value over the next two years. Within a few years I came to the realization that the world is frequently irrational, people are usually impatient, and being humbled is part of the curriculum in the school of life. Unfortunately, none of these supports a long-term investment perspective.

"What Have You Done for Me Lately?"

A headline grabbing example of how investors' unrelenting demand for instant performance can reach absurd levels occurred in the second quarter of 1996. Jeffrey Vinik, manager of the largest and most closely watched mutual fund, Fidelity Magellan Fund, abruptly resigned after posting a below average return for the first four months of 1996. While the reason for his resignation was not completely clear, his fund's underperformance presumably played a significant role. The fact that his 17.2 percent average return over nearly four years beat most of his competition was of little consequence. Vinik's underperformance was due to his belief that a conservative posture was most prudent in a market that was overvalued by most measures.[31] The pressure for instant performance was never more obvious. This also illustrates why a company that has to report quarterly to its stockholders and needs to raise capital periodically in the public market feels so much pressure to meet or exceed earnings projections. The emphasis on near-term performance often means that long-term objectives are disregarded or jeopardized.

Due, among other things, to investors' obsessive focus on short-term performance, it is not easy for a corporation to combine a superior earnings record and socially responsible business practices. Hewlett-Packard, with revenues exceeding $38 billion and an unleveraged 20 percent return on equity, appears to be one of the exceptions. It has achieved its considerable success without disruptive restructurings and, unlike most of today's corporate behemoths, without significant layoffs. Even in the recession of 1970, it asked its employees to take a 10 percent pay cut and was, thereby, able to avoid pink slips. While IBM has shed a large percentage of its workforce in the last ten years, HP has twenty thousand more employees worldwide than it had a decade ago. What are the secrets to their two-pronged success? Unlike the top down hierarchical structure of most traditional corporations, Hewlett-Packard has always had a more egalitarian structure, where individuals at all levels could exercise their abilities to the utmost. Lewis Platt, the Chief Executive Officer of HP, does not talk about running the company. As he tells it:

> I spend a lot of my time talking about values rather than trying to figure out the business strategies. The most important aspect of the management of this company is cultural control.[32]

Decentralization and openness are two hallmarks of the HP organization. There are no executive offices, just low partitions with an opening on one side and no doors. Dress is informal with suits the exception. Thinking long-term is another very important aspect of their success. Research and development spending is emphasized; in one year they plowed $2.7 billion into the company's R&D effort. To put this in perspective, their R&D expenditures represented 7 percent of sales and exceeded net profits of some $2.5 billion.[33]

While CEO Lewis Platt is not a high-profile corporate celebrity, his value-driven leadership is widely recognized and admired. Fortune magazine's 1995 survey of America's Most Admired Companies ranked HP in the top ten.[34] And in a poll of 497 chief executives, conducted by the Gallup Organization, Lewis Platt was ranked fourth out of a select list of twelve chief executives whose companies have had exceptional records over the past five years.[35] Hewlett-Packard is a stellar example of how it is possible to be both financially successful and socially responsible. When the chief executive places values at the top of the company's priorities, all things are possible.

With respect to influence from the top, a May 1996 conference on corporate citizenship, called for and presided over by the President of the United States, is certainly worth noting. With over one hundred corporate executives in attendance, President Clinton began the panel discussions with the following statement:

> What I want to see us do is to elevate the good practices that are going on, show how they are consistent with making money and succeeding in the free enterprise system, and hope that we can reinforce that kind of conduct that so many of you have brought to bear in your own companies and with your own employees.[36]

Clinton put forth his view of the traits a good corporate citizen should possess:

- They should be family-friendly, helping workers care for elderly parents or attend parent-teacher meetings.
- They should offer a living wage, health benefits and retirement security.
- They should provide a safe and secure workplace.

- They should invest in their employees' education and training.
- They should listen to employees' needs and concerns. When layoffs are necessary they should be as fair and helpful to the displaced worker as possible.

The President also announced the Ron Brown Corporate Citizenship Award which goes to the company that best achieves these goals on an annual basis.[37]

There is little doubt that this type of event encourages companies that are at the forefront of these activities to continue their innovation and caring behavior. It is also likely to get the attention of those companies that have been slow to reevaluate their objectives in light of the changing needs of their many constituencies. Pronouncements from the top, whether it be the CEO of a corporation or the head of the government, do have an impact on getting the populace to reflect on important issues that will shape society in the years to come.

RESISTING THE RESISTANCE TO CHANGE

The idea that business is responsible for more than maximizing profits is not yet the prevalent view. While the pressures cited above will change this situation over time, there is another factor which, when recognized, may quicken the pace of the transformation. As a member of the human race, each person shares in all the beauty and sorrow of life. We accept advanced computers, digital cellular telephones, the Internet, air conditioning and even indoor plumbing as our birthright because we are part of a civilization which has created these products. We share in these inventions even though few of us have made any direct contribution to the actual creation of these conveniences. They accrue to us because we happen to be part of a particular culture that has inherited them. On the other hand, when faced with inequality, poverty, disease, crime and pollution, too many people refuse to take responsibility for this phase of the cultural pattern.

Yet they are very much our responsibility as they are also aspects of our heredity.

It is well to remember that The Principle of Cause and Effect holds that a relationship exists between everything that has gone before and everything that follows. This is more commonly known as Newton's third law of motion; for every action (i.e., force) there is an equal and opposite reaction. Mystics say that this rule which applies to the physical world also holds true on emotional and mental levels and is often referred to as the law of karma. Karma is a Sanskrit word that implies that action is always balanced by a corresponding reaction. The American Indians expressed much the same understanding in the aphorism:

> In our every deliberation, we must consider the impact of our decisions on the next seven generations. (From the Great Law of the Iroquois Confederacy.)

Some people think they can make the same mistake over and over yet somehow obtain better results. Hermes frowns upon such lunacy; his teachings explicitly decreed that knowledge is of little value unless expressed in action. Be wary of mental miserliness and put into practice all that you learn, was one of his cardinal messages.[38] Businesses are obliged to accept responsibility and take corrective actions as soon as they become aware of a problem. To do anything less is not only morally and ethically questionable but, according to the law of causation, will have disturbing effects. If corrective action is not taken to close the hole in the ozone, for example, the generations that ignore the warnings will face the consequences just as surely as they will benefit from the money currently being spent on advanced space and medical research.

To summarize, when a business recognizes that it is a living organization composed of, and interacting with, living organisms (employees, customers, suppliers, neighbors and owners), it will feel compelled to act responsibly. It will recognize, either explicitly or implicitly, the omnipresent law of cause and effect.

It will learn to accept and appreciate the often hidden justice that is inherent in every aspect of life. All goals and objectives will have a long-term, broad-based focus. Those enterprises that have not accepted this new paradigm of old wisdom will begin to do so as pressure is brought to bear from many directions. Business support for a holistic model of the world, with all its ramifications, may occur sooner than currently imagined. When it does, a critical threshold can be achieved that will facilitate the movement toward a higher level of consciousness for all humanity.

In the next chapter we will look at some of the ways society is regenerating itself as a result of the policies and actions of the individuals and businesses that have been in the forefront of this transformation.

NOTES

1. H. B. Fuller Company. *1996 Annual Report* (St. Paul, MN), p. 38.

2. Ibid, p. 2.

3. Kristen Baird. "Modern Family Concerns Show up in Company Policies," *Small Business News* (Philadelphia), December 1994, p. 30.

4. Marjorie Kelly. "The President as Poet: An Intimate Conversation with Jim Autry," in *The New Paradigm in Business: Emerging Strategies for Leadership and Organizational Change*, ed. Michael Ray and Alan Rinzler (New York: Putnam Publishing Group for the World Business Academy, 1993), p. 96.

5. "CEO Sees Business as the Engine for Social Transformation," *The New Leaders*, January/February 1995, p. 3.

6. "French Executive Scouts for New Business Ideas," *The New Leaders*, November/December 1995, p. 12.

7. William H. Lee, R.Ph., *Coenzyme Q-10: Is it our New Fountain of Youth?*, A Good Health Guide, ed. Richard A. Passwater, Ph.D. and Earl Mindell, R.Ph., Ph.D. (New Canaan, CT: Keats Publishing, 1987), p. 1.

8. Bristol-Myers Squibb Company, *1994 Annual Report* (New York), p. 18.

9. Ibid.

10. Ken Baskin. "Is Your Business Alive?" *Business Philadelphia*, November 1994, p. 18.

11. Ellen Galinsky and Peter J. Stein. "The Impact of Human Resource Policies on Employees: Balancing Work/Family Life," *Journal of Family Issues* 11 (December 1990), p. 380.

12. Sue Shellenbarger. "Work & Family," *Wall Street Journal*, 1 March 1995, p. 1(B).

13. Dana E. Friedman and Ellen Galinsky. *Work and Family Trends* (New York: Families and Work Institute, 1991), p. 2.

14. *Women: The New Providers* (New York: Families and Work Institute, 1995), pp. 11, 66, 70, 86, 90–91.

15. Burton G. Malkiel. "Socially Responsible Investing," in *Classics II: Another Investor's Anthology*, ed. Charles D. Ellis with James R. Vertin (Homewood, IL: Business One Irwin, 1991), p. 604.

16. "1997 Report on Responsible Investing Trends in the United States," Washington, DC, 5 November 1997; available from http://www.socialinvest.org; accessed January 2, 1998.

17. James K. Glassman. "'Ethical' Stocks Don't Have to Be Downers," *Washington Post*, 23 April 1995, p. 1(H).

18. Peter Kinder, Steven D. Lydenberg, and Amy L. Domini. *Investing for Good: Making Money While Being Socially Responsible* (New York: HarperCollins, 1993), pp. 29–31.

19. David Rudnick. "Cents & Sensibility," *Business Life: The Magazine for Europe*, February 1997, p. 53.

20. Judith H. Dobrzynski, "An Inside Look at CalPERS Boardroom Report Card," *Business Week*, 17 October 1994, p. 196.

21. Asra Q. Nomani. "CalPERS Says Its Investment Decisions Will Reflect How Firms Treat Workers," *Wall Street Journal*, 16 June 1994, p. 6(A). Reprinted by permission of *Wall Street Journal*, © 1994 Dow Jones and Company, Inc. All Rights Reserved Worldwide.

22. Ibid.

23. John J. Fried. "Saving the Earth, and They Mean Business," *Philadelphia Inquirer*, 18 December 1994, p. 1(M).

24. Rosemary Brown, ed., *Co-op America's National Green Pages*™ (Washington: Co-op America, 1996), p. 33.

25. *Compass: The Newsletter of The Natural Step* 2 (Fall 1996), p. 6.

26. *The Natural Step Community Seminar Brochure*, 16 June 1997.

27. *Business for Social Responsibility Fact Sheet* (San Francisco, May 1997).

28. Russell Mitchell with Michael Oneal. "Managing by Values: Is Levi Strauss' Approach Visionary—or Flaky?" *Business Week*, 1 August 1994, p. 46.

29. Martha Groves and Stuart Silverstein, "Levi Strauss Tailors a Deal to Suit its Workers," *Philadelphia Inquirer*, 7 June 1996, p. 2(C).

30. Tom's Of Maine. *The Common Good Report 1994* (Kennebunk, ME), pp. 5, 7, 10.

31. John Greenwald. "Magellan's New Direction," *Time*, 3 June 1996, p. 56.

32. Dana Wechsler Linden and Bruce Upbin. "Boy Scouts on a Rampage," *Forbes*, 1 January 1996, p. 67.

33. Hewlett-Packard Company. *Hewlett-Packard in Brief 1997* (Palo Alto, CA, April 1997), p. 4.

34. Stratford Sherman. "Secrets of HP's 'Muddled' Team," *Fortune*, 18 March 1996, p. 116.

35. Linden and Upbin, p. 70.

36. "Conference on Corporate Citizenship," Washington, DC, 16 May 1996; available from the White House Virtual Library, http://www.whitehouse.gov; accessed 7 June 1997.

37. "Good Citizens," *Investor's Business Daily*, 17 May 1996, p. 1(B).

38. Three Initiates, pp. 213–214.

7

Profiting from Inclusion

Once it is recognized that a business is a living organization, management's obligations become multidimensional. Profitability must share the spotlight with holistic values. Unwavering commitment to ethical behavior, heartfelt concern for the community at large, respect for differences of all kinds and the need for balanced and sustainable long-term growth are principles that provide a framework within which all parties find enrichment, growth and prosperity. We have previously shown how ethical/responsible corporate behavior can, in fact, bolster the bottom line. For further support of this position consider the following:

- In 1996, Marriott International began offering its 185,000 employees (80% of whom earn about $7 an hour) a variety of services, almost none directly related to the performance of their jobs. The employees were given professional assistance with such things as immigration and domestic abuse issues, auto loans, elder care, and housing concerns. The company claims a minimum five-to-one return on the money spent on the counseling services in the form of reduced turnover, absenteeism and tardiness. In addition, they see significant positive, but unquantifiable, benefits such as increased morale, company loyalty and productivity.[1]

- Dow Chemical announced plans to spend $1 billion, through 2005, on a set of environmental initiatives. According to William Stavropoulos, Dow's president and chief executive officer: "Companies who want to thrive in the next century will manage for global competitiveness, in large part by reducing wastes, cutting emissions and preventing incidents. In the new world, where all markets are open, inefficient and poorly-managed plants will be obsolete . . . we expect a 30 to 40 percent return on this investment."[2]

- In a study conducted by Cone Communications and Roper Starch Worldwide 31 percent of respondents felt that a company's sense of social responsibility was a major factor in their purchasing decisions. Fifty-four percent of adults stated they would pay more for a product that supported a cause in which they were interested. In addition, a survey of 2500 business students, conducted by Students for Responsible Business, found that two thirds would take lower salaries to work for socially responsible employers.[3]

And, in a monumental effort to advance the understanding of gender and family concerns and their impact on a variety of non-work issues, the Ford Foundation, beginning in 1990, entered into a research partnership with three companies: Corning, Xerox and Tandem Computers. The joint objective was to study whether the incorporation of certain systemic changes in the way work was done would enable employees to integrate their work and personal lives more efficiently without a negative effect on business goals. A positive report of the findings was issued at the end of 1996. According to Paul Allaire, CEO of Xerox:

> The project began with the belief that changes in work practices that were designed to make work and the workplace more family-friendly could be accomplished with no loss to business productivity. But this view underestimated the benefits of a

work-family approach. The research shows that this approach offers companies a strategic opportunity to achieve a more equitable and a more productive workplace . . . it is gratifying that this study has established that the best business strategy recognizes that greater employee satisfaction means greater productivity and, in turn, better business results.[4]

Robert H. Rosen Ph.D., author, consultant and recipient of a MacArthur Foundation grant to research new models of work for the year 2000, describes the part values play in a healthy company as follows:

> . . . values are perpetually interacting, expanding, and contracting like a living entity. Each value depends on and determines the health of the others; sickness or disease that undermines one weakens all; robustness in one value strengthens all. The values at the heart of a company enable it to continuously grow, evolve, and renew itself, reinforcing what is productive and positive and sloughing off the unhealthy and unworkable. In short, the causes and effects between values, people, and companies are not linear but circular. Values are the center of the enterprise; they circulate through every cell and artery of a company, and a company and its employees either reinforce values or bring about their decline.[5]

The human spirit cannot flourish if parts of the organization are treated inequitably or if the surrounding environment is abused or degraded. The only way to be certain that a business is progressing toward its full potential is to establish and enforce policies that fully consider the intrinsic needs of all who are affected by the organization's decisions. Some of the agents for change were described in the last chapter. In addition, women, in growing numbers and of all races and regions, are at the forefront of this workplace metamorphosis and are earning respect and recognition for their contributions. This chapter, therefore, begins with a detailed look at the transformative role women are playing throughout society and then goes on to discuss the ramifications that necessarily flow from the reinvigoration of this vital center of influence.

THE VENUS RENEWAL

According to author Ken Wilber, whose writings on the evolution of consciousness have been compared to Freud's pioneering work in psychology, a worldwide shift from a matriarchal to a patriarchal society occurred around the second or third millennium B. C.[6] This transformation coincided with an evolutionary change from dominance of the body to that of the mind. At the time, the female/mother image was relegated to the birth-body-earth realm, and the emerging mental culture came under the domain of the male/father. Through a combination of happenstance and outright exploitation, a preferential status of the masculine evolved.[7] As described in chapter two, The Principle of Gender proclaims that humans have both masculine and feminine qualities embedded in their personalities. The following is a list of some of the characteristics attributed to each of these elements:

Masculine	*Feminine*
rational	intuitive
projective	receptive
active	passive
initiating	elaborating, enlarging
force	form
analytic, classifying, separating	synthetic, healing, unifying
self-conscious, observant	subconscious, instinctive

It is appropriate to examine where society currently stands in its quest to equalize the masculine and feminine elements. According to Ken Wilber:

... as the male once rescued consciousness from the chthonic matriarchate, the female might today help rescue consciousness—and her brother—from patriarchate. And as the innate but initial masculine mode seemed appropriate for the former, the innate but initial feminine mode seems appropriate for the latter. We of today face a new dragon fight, and we need a new Hero Myth. ... We need today to develop intuition and alert but passive awareness, as we yesterday needed so desperately to develop assertive logic and active mentality. The new Hero will be ... whole-bodied, mentally androgynous, psychic, intuitive *and* rational, male *and* female—and the lead in this new development most easily can come *from* the female, since our society is *already* masculine-adapted.[8]

A great deal has happened since those words were written in 1981; women (who, generally speaking, possess a preponderance of the feminine element) are having an increasingly significant influence on all aspects of our society. This is no more evident than in the world of business. More than a third of entrepreneurs are women and some 570 women serve on corporate boards of the Fortune 500, compared with forty-six in 1977. But it has not been easy; women around the world have had to struggle to make it in the workplace.

Age old gender stereotypes have not disappeared and continue to make it difficult for women to get equal-handed treatment. Polls indicate that there is still a large segment of the population, both male and female, that think the husband should be the breadwinner and the wife should stay at home. The percentage of people agreeing with this belief ranged from a high of 56 percent in Japan to a low of 13 percent in Sweden. In America, Britain, France and Germany the agreement ranged between 20 and 25 percent. It should be noted that Sweden's pro-family policies are among the most generous in the world, including year-long paid maternity and paternity leaves, lengthy vacations, free day care and job protection. Approximately 85 percent of Swedish women work for 77 percent of the wages earned by men (higher than in most countries). Nonetheless, they are largely absent from top management, holding only 8 percent of private-sector managerial jobs.[9]

Women may actually be making the most progress in post-communist satellites such as the former East Germany. Compared to western Germany, where 38 percent of women work, 94 percent of eastern Germany's adult women were working prior to reunification. As a result, many of the women have managerial skills and have launched nearly one-third of all new businesses since 1990 compared to 21 percent in western Germany. Interestingly, researchers who have studied this new business growth have found that the profit motive is not as pronounced among women entrepreneurs as it is among men. Women, in the United States as well as eastern Germany, put earning profits fourth or fifth behind such things as the desire to be self-sufficient and develop their own ideas. Men, in contrast, usually cite profits as their prime motivation.[10] Whatever the impetus, women worldwide are beginning to assert their rights in the workplace. While equilibrium has not yet been achieved, recent progress has been both intellectually and pragmatically welcome. Judy Wicks, president of the highly acclaimed restaurant, the White Dog Cafe, and a recipient of the prestigious Business Enterprise Award, describes some of the contributions women make when they become valued members of the workforce:

> Despite the prejudicial treatment, women of my generation have not only proven that we can succeed in the marketplace, but more importantly we are helping change the very nature of capitalism. While our male counterparts were taught win-lose competition and a success-at-any-cost approach to business, girls with an eye toward child rearing and homemaking learned to see life holistically . . . we recognize that we cannot compartmentalize our lives as men have practiced. The same values apply in the workplace and at home where we teach our children to treat others as we would like them to treat us. . . . Our natural environment and our local world communities cannot be sacrificed or neglected for the sake of short-term profit. A successful economic system is inclusive. In the end, we cannot win while

others lose, and the entrepreneurial energies of all people will create a world where everyone profits, the air and water are clean, and economic justice eliminates the need for war. We are practicing capitalism for the common good, and we have what it takes.[11]

These comments echo the more general concerns and priorities of the women interviewed for a Whirlpool Foundation study. When asked about their priorities, they said that they are most concerned with creating a more caring environment in the home, at work, among all families and in society at large.[12] In addition, the women stated that they encourage their children to spend time with people of diverse social, economic and ethnic backgrounds.[13] These feelings clearly reflect the feminine components of nurturing, healing and unifying. According to Carol R. Frenier, author of *Business and the Feminine Principle: The Untapped Resource:*

> I believe that the way we collectively relate to each other is also the substance of our current revolution, and that the feminine principle has much to contribute to this effort to evolve to an even higher, more participatory form of organization—in our homes, our businesses, and in our government.[14]

A more participatory form of management, such as the open book management structure discussed in chapter five, would certainly get Hermes' approval. The Hermetic Principles describe a universe that is inexorably united. The interdependent nature of such a reality necessitates a cooperative/cocreative spirit in all our relationships. Dominating, non-inclusive forms of leadership are clearly counterproductive as they are unable to garner wide support or tap the full potential of a heterogeneous group of participants. Women's rising influence in business is likely to bring greater attention to the need for a more diverse workforce where everyone can contribute.

As humanity matures, we can expect to transcend the unhealthy state that exists when there is a disproportionate amount

of either male or female qualities, replacing it with a new androgynous personality that melds the two together.[15] As expressed by
Jungian psychologist June Singer, Ph.D.:

> The androgyne sees the overriding principle of union, acting
> continually to overcome separation, and knows that the separa-
> tion is as essential to life as the union. . . . Androgyny demands
> the freedom to function out of one side of our nature or the other
> as a dominant way of being; yet androgyny recognizes the re-
> sponsibility to be aware that there is always the other side as
> well, which needs to be taken into account in the long-range
> movement toward union.[16]

DIVERSITY REGENERATES

Since the Civil Rights Act of 1964 and the subsequent installation
of affirmative action programs, the number of women and minorities in the workplace has been steadily growing. In the mid-
1990s, minorities accounted for up to 23 percent of the workforce
versus 10.7 percent in 1964; women make up nearly half the managerial and professional ranks. Most large companies have become true believers in a rainbow workforce not just because it is
equitable but also because such diversity presents a breadth of
experiences and ideas. Input from a variety of sources can be crucial when dealing with a wide range of customers, both culturally
and geographically.[17] Yet Taylor Cox, who studies minorities in
corporations, has conducted studies that show that minorities
and women quit companies 2.5 times as often as white males.[18]
When it costs upwards of $150,000 to train a professional em-
ployee, employers do not want to see that investment wasted.
Turnover can be the result of many causes; too often it is attributable to cultural prejudices. Women may not be given timely
promotions, Hispanics may feel isolated, African-Americans are
often stereotyped in certain types of jobs, Asians may find themselves pigeonholed in research and development. Unaddressed
cultural problems can lead to widespread dissension, decrease

worker productivity and make recruiting of minorities more difficult. According to consultant and author Carol Sanford:

> We developed a wide array of fine-tuned and costly instruments for categorizing, classifying, and segmenting the performance of people. We take almost any process that could help us understand the totality of ourselves individually and collectively and convert it to a segmenting tool. As a result we are losing, or have lost, the valuing of diversity needed to gain wholeness and to support the heterostatic processes of regeneration required to survive in our rapidly changing environment.[19]

Recognizing the need for a workforce that not only reflects the diversity of the population but one that acts as a harmonious team, many corporations have established entire departments with large budgets to set and monitor corporate diversity policies. Some companies now base part of a manager's bonus on whether divisional diversity goals are met. While there is certainly room for improvement, a reasonable case can be made that the momentum toward equality in the workforce will not be slowed even if governmental pressure subsides. As stated by GTE in its annual report, ". . . dedication to diversity and equal opportunity is a matter of values, not legislation."[20]

Illustrative of what can be done when a company decides to go beyond legal mandates and really get to the heart of the problem is a program set up by United Parcel Service (UPS). In order to create a meaningful program, the company turned to Walter Hooke who had begun his career at UPS as a consultant. Hooke recognized that simply changing hiring practices for front-line, entry-level workers would not solve the root causes of the problem. Without changing the attitudes of the managers who supervised their diverse workforce, progress toward a more tolerant corporate culture would be surface level at best. With the support of top management Hooke began a Community Internship Program. He believed that being aware of an issue is not the same as being actively involved in doing something about it. This mandatory program takes upper- and middle-level managers off the job for one month and puts them through an internship that sensitizes them to people who come from very different backgrounds and circumstances. Forty managers are chosen annually and placed in one of a number of sites.

Interns are given the responsibility of overseeing a little brother or sister. During their month of service they also interact with a wide variety of people ranging from illegal immigrants to disadvantaged elderly. They may go to prisons, ride in police cars, meet with social service organizations, talk to AIDS patients, help drug addicts or help the homeless. Both the intern and the community benefit from the association. In one case, interns discovered that a majority of a local clinic's budget was spent on purifying contaminated drinking water. They proposed new methods to clean up the water and saved the clinic a significant amount of money. Disadvantaged people get to experience first hand that a large corporation cares about more than just the bottom line. Most managers come away with a more compassionate view of their fellow human beings and a greater appreciation for whatever blessings they have received. They often become more involved in their own communities as they begin to realize one person can truly make a difference.

The program costs UPS about $10,000 per intern, approximately $400,000 annually. Although it is difficult to quantify the payback from this program, the company cites such benefits as reduced grievances, improved relations with the community and a very low 2 percent turnover rate among their managers as tangible evidence that the program has been advantageous. Today most managers are anxious to participate in an internship as part of their career development plan.[21] But perhaps the best indication of the program's success can be found in a letter Aileen Hernandez, the first women to sit on the Equal Employment Opportunities Commission and a founding member of the National Organization of Women, wrote to Hooke upon his retirement:

I have watched a steady, and sometimes dramatic, change of attitude and behavior that has made it possible for me to name UPS as one of the few companies in the nation which I believe has actually institutionalized the concept of equal employment opportunity. . . . Your approach has been deceptively simple—you have focused on the people developing skills in your managers and have incorporated into their training some interaction with 'nontraditional' people. Your intern program is an outstanding example of this, and the words of the participants themselves substantiate the value of having them 'walk in someone else's shoes' for a while.[22]

AN ECOLOGICAL REJUVENATION

The words ecology and economy come from the same Greek root, *oikos*, meaning home. Our home is planet earth. Our bodily existence, during our sojourn on Gaia, is dependent upon the air we breathe, the water we drink and the food that nourishes us. If our land, atmosphere or waterways are polluted, we function at less than optimum levels, eventually leading to disabling diseases and/or premature death. Until recently, most businesses failed to see the connection between their first priority, making money, and the needs of the surrounding environment. The overriding objective was to enhance short-term profits which, among other things, meant holding down costs, particularly expenses that are seemingly nonproductive. The fact that this shortsighted approach was possibly detrimental to society at large was of little concern; that it was inimical to long-term profitability, ignored. As it became more apparent that business was courting disaster with its wasteful and destructive environmental practices, concerned citizens spoke out and governmental authorities stepped in. In 1969, the United States Congress passed the National Environmental Policy Act which declared that the federal government has a responsibility to restore and maintain a wholesome environment. In addition, an Environmental Impact Statement was required to assess any proposed legislation or project that might have a deleterious effect on ecological quality.[23]

While coercive government regulations are a costly and cumbersome way to effect change, they do force the regulated entity to pay close attention to the problem. How has business handled its environmental responsibilities after more than a quarter century of expanded and, some would argue, onerous oversight? According to Price Waterhouse, which surveys approximately thirteen hundred businesses about their environmental practices every two years, boardrooms across the nation are behaving "green" in growing numbers. Since 1990, the percentage of companies with guidelines that account for environmental costs has grown from 11 percent to 63 percent. Many businesses are conducting environmental audits that assess how well they are complying with environmental regulations and their own pollution prevention policies. In fact, almost 40 percent of the companies surveyed include managers' environmental performance in the formula used to determine compensation.[24] This is more than a case of unbridled altruism or a guilty social conscience; cutting down on pollution can reduce future legal liabilities and insurance costs. And recycling, whether it is waste paper, packaging, the product itself or equipment the company no longer wants, can save big money.

WASTE IS A TERRIBLE THING TO MIND

Minnesota Mining and Manufacturing Company (3M) has an internationally recognized program, called Pollution Prevention Pays (3P), which solicits employee suggestions on how to cut waste, recycle materials and prevent pollution at the source. Since its inception in 1975, employees have generated more than four thousand ideas that have prevented 750,000 tons of air, water and solid waste pollutants. The program has saved 3M more than $790 million by eliminating sources of pollution. In addition to reducing pollution, productivity has been enhanced and the effects of raw material price increases minimized. Breakthroughs by 3M in pollution prevention technologies have led to a number of innovative products. 3P has been praised around the world by environmental organizations, government officials and the United Nations and has been copied by a number of companies.[25]

The movement to recycle corporate assets is called investment recovery and simply mirrors what families have done for years—passing on things no longer needed. In fact, the whole recycling effort is a reflection of natural laws followed since time began. Recycling conserves resources and environmentally correct corporate policies enable consumers and employees alike to feel better about the enterprise with which they are associated. Increasingly, some corporate waste is finding its way to nonprofit community groups in the form of donated materials. It is a perfect example of a win/win/win strategy. The community gets something of value, company benefits vary from simple goodwill to reduced disposal costs and/or a tax deduction and the environment is spared wasted resources and potential pollution problems.

Warner Brothers Burbank Studios and 20th Century Fox have developed a "community reuse partnership" called Second Time Around that takes this concept to the nth degree. Their alliance has identified specific nonprofit organizations that are ready, willing and able to make use of the studios' surplus goods. They have established a proprietary data base that lists hundreds of schools, hospitals, theater and arts groups, health clinics, environmental organizations and other nonprofit groups in their region. The database lists each organization's purpose, preferred goods, transportation availability and contact information. Whenever something becomes expendable, the staff can quickly find the most appropriate recipient and arrange for distribution. In one three-month period there were thirty-one donations to sixteen different groups. This included more than five tons worth of computers, refrigerators, bookcases, lumber, paint, etc. that would otherwise have been sent to landfills.

Other companies, particularly smaller ones, have implemented scaled down versions of a recycled donations program. The thirty-five employees at Crib Diaper Service near Minneapolis discovered that art students could use some of the laundry's 600 cubic yards of cotton lint to make art paper. Some organizations, such as Material for the Arts in Atlanta and the Artscrap Resource Center in St. Paul, turn donations into raw materials for art projects. Many restaurants regularly donate food to organizations servicing homeless shelters and soup kitchens. Foodchain: The Association of Prepared and Perishable Food Rescue Programs is a national clearinghouse which helps companies donate excess food to nonprofits. The Reuse Development Organization is being established to connect various community reuse programs. Its goal is to help businesses find appropriate recipients for their contributions on a nationwide basis just as Warner/Fox has accomplished on a regional scale.[26] The growth of these programs is encouraging.

This trend toward greater corporate responsibility is a worldwide phenomenon. A network of international business leaders, The Business Leaders Forum, was established to promote the idea that good corporate citizenship helps maintain the global environment and, thereby, improves everyone's quality of life.[27] This group publishes a report entitled "Corporate Community Involvement" highlighting emerging trends; governments around the world are getting the message. Many like-minded groups are active in Europe and elsewhere.

CRADLE TO GRAVE

Although most companies base new product decisions strictly on marketing and financial analyses, many now include an assessment of potential environmental, health and safety risks in their product planning deliberations. Such an approach provides a more comprehensive picture upon which to calculate a product's ultimate profitability. By making this analysis an integral part of the design, manufacturing, distribution, product use, recycling and disposal process, all costs can be factored into the marketing and pricing equation. To make an accurate life-cycle assessment requires the active participation and cooperation of not only environmental and health and safety specialists but financial, marketing and manufacturing personnel as well.

While extra time and effort may be expended during the product development process, these initiatives improve the quality of products, packaging and processes, avoid negative public relations and contribute to the company's long-term prosperity. Life-cycle analysis is a good example of how business is using an feminine attribute—that of synthesizing—rather than the more traditional approach of looking at individual parts and giving little if any thought to future ramifications.

One of the most progressive companies on the environmental front is Polaroid Corporation. Back in 1977, the company published a policy statement on the environment. It states in part:

> Polaroid's goal is to carry on our industrial activity in harmony with the natural ecosystems so as to achieve the minimum adverse effect on land, air and water quality. . . . Environmental protection is a continuing responsibility of each individual and all functions of the Company. We recognize expenses for environmental protection as an appropriate cost of doing business and we will assign qualified people the responsibility and authority to achieve our environmental goals.[28]

The values and principles reflected in this policy include individual and corporate responsibility, strict standards for environmental performance, source reduction, recycling and resource conservation. They are implemented through Polaroid's Toxic Use and Waste Reduction program adopted for the entire company in 1988. It was also in that year that Polaroid became the first United States company to publish an annual environmental report. This forty-plus page public report assesses progress and challenges in three broad environmental areas: toxic use and waste reduction, environmental stewardship and community involvement. In addition, in 1994 they joined four other Fortune 500 companies that had previously endorsed the *CERES PRINCIPLES*, a code of environmental conduct that is discussed in detail later in the book. The philosophy underlying all these actions is that "Polaroid has a fundamental ethical responsibility to protect the environment, and that the dual goals of good corporate citizenship and good business are eminently compatible."[29]

As other businesses catch up with those at the forefront of the environmental effort, our planet will begin a period of rejuvenation that can bring the ecosystem back to the pristine state of balance that humankind has long since forgotten. The success that has been achieved in reclaiming some of our rivers and lakes is but a glimpse of what is possible once all citizens begin to take their responsibilities seriously.

PUSHING AND PULLING TOWARD EQUILIBRIUM

All of the changes we have been discussing—the reascendancy of the feminine element, the acknowledgment that diversity is both necessary and desirable and the recognition that the environment must be fully respected—have been gradually and, in some cases, grudgingly accepted largely because of government regulation. Affirmative action requirements and environmental protection mandates have forced businesses to reexamine their personnel policies and disposal practices and make more socially responsible decisions. As is always the case, we may now be at a point where the balance is shifting from an extreme position at one end of the spectrum toward a equally unhealthy bias in the other direction. Some feminist groups are reactivating "female only" matriarchal obsessions, cases of blatant reverse discrimination have become increasingly common and environmental activists have employed extreme tactics in the name of their nature-loving cause. At the same time, the high costs and inefficiencies of many bureaucratic regulations are diluting the government's ability to accomplish what was originally intended.

Superfund legislation provides a graphic illustration of how good intentions can quickly go awry. The United States Congress created Superfund in 1980 to pay for the cleanup of chemical waste sites. During the ensuing years, over thirteen hundred sites have been placed on Superfund's National Priorities List. The Superfund has now expended more than thirty billion dollars. Despite these enormous outlays, relatively few sites have been removed from the list; some should never have been listed in the first place. Where did all the money go? The Dallas-based National Center for Policy Analysis reported that between thirty-six and sixty cents of every Superfund dollar goes to pay legal costs. This depressingly inefficient use of taxpayer money can be attributed, at least in part, to questionable standards of liability set up under the law.

Termed "joint-and-several liability," this statute means that any party associated with the site can be forced to pay for the entire cleanup and often results in trying to collect from current owners even though they were never involved in polluting the site. Costly, time-consuming lawsuits are the inevitable result. In addition, the law requires that specific cleanup technologies be used even if other less costly alternatives are available. Setting and enforcing standards is an appropriate function of the EPA. Deciding how standards should be met, however, simply delays the cleanup while the parties haggle over the shape of the table. Finally, many feel that the EPA insists on standards of cleanliness that go beyond what is necessary or reasonable. Case in point: the EPA concluded that one site was a risk based on the assumption that a child playing at the site would eat two hundred milligrams of dirt each and every day for seventy years. The fact that few people past early childhood are likely to be attracted to dirt, much less interested in eating it, did not seem to prevent the EPA from concluding that unless their standards were met, health would be endangered.[30]

As this example makes obvious, laws that were originally made to protect society can all too often end up doing more harm than good. In this regard, a recently published environmental law treatise stated, "It is virtually impossible for a major company (or government facility) to be in complete compliance with all regulatory requirements. [And yet] virtually every instance of noncompliance can be readily translated into a [criminal] violation."[31]

Unfortunately, our legislatures seem oblivious to the situation; outmoded laws are usually revised and supplemented rather than repealed.

Complicated and contradictory affirmative action regulations also present companies with "Solomon-like" dilemmas. Quotas are illegal but numerical goals are acceptable. A business is expected to increase the number of minorities in its workforce but breaks the law if it reserves a job until a qualified minority applicant is found. Just about everyone is part of a protected class. Laws now include protection for anyone over forty years of age as well as those with a disability. Meanwhile drug addicts are arguing that they too should be given extra consideration because they are disabled.[32] Since the early 1970s we have seen the pendulum swing from one extreme to an equally untenable position at the opposite pole.

Cycles are an intrinsic part of life with a perpetual ebb and flow clearly embedded in the evolutionary process. The Principle of Rhythm tells us that we are continually moving; first toward a position on one end of the spectrum and then reversing course and heading for the other extreme. There is always an advance and a retreat, a rising and a sinking, an action and a reaction. Stars, planets, people, animals, plants, minerals, energy and consciousness all follow this Principle. The Principle of Rhythm accounts for the creation and destruction of celestial objects, the rise and fall of nations and the mental states of humanity. Recurrent cyclic patterns are a requisite condition wherever there is duality. Repeated alternation between two poles is necessary as it produces a discomfort sufficient to motivate us to equilibrate the pairs of opposites and thereby gain a sense of peace and fulfillment. *All of our lessons are directly related to the same fundamental problem; we think and act as if we were separate entities rather than unalterably united with all of creation.* If all our actions were in concert with and in recognition of the unity and interdependence of life, we would have never degraded the environment or disadvantaged any of the seemingly different members of the human species. We are given the opportunity to view the landscape from varying angles until eventually, after innumerable rhythmic repetitions, the light dawns and we move toward a state of equilibrium.

Once the lesson is learned, policies established to resolve the problem must be made a permanent part of any institution. Doing so ensures that future responses are not dependent upon a specific leader or a temporary directive that can be easily replaced or distorted. The process of rhythmic repetition patterns our subconscious so that our reactions become automatic. This is what ageless wisdom and the perennial philosophy call mastery, and it is a goal that can only be attained with practice, patience and persistence. When mastery is achieved in one area as, for example, proper treatment of the environment, the cumbersome and often counterproductive laws that were originally needed to regulate these particular abuses can be relaxed or, even better, eliminated. For governments to do otherwise risks the pendulum swinging to the other extreme and causing unintended consequences, not the least of which is negating the gains previously attained.

To recap, in a competitive business environment often characterized by downsizing and restructuring, it is essential that employees be motivated, creative and loyal. Cultivating such a workforce is largely dependent on a code of ethics which deals honestly with and respects all parties regardless of their cultural background or socioeconomic class. When a company's values are widely disseminated and strictly enforced, a socially responsible organization is the natural result. The growing influence of the feminine element is accelerating the movement toward a more sensitive and compassionate business environment. In such an atmosphere, turnover is minimized and productivity enhanced. A heightened level of *esprit de corps* is likely to develop and produce a revitalized and rejuvenated organization. In the words of best-selling author and management expert, Kenneth H. Blanchard, Ph.D.:

Other benefits of being ethical are more psychological in nature. At the individual level [living organism], being ethical has a positive effect on self-esteem; at the organizational level [living organization], being ethical helps to build and maintain company pride.[33]

It will take time before the magnitude of the societal transformation currently underway is clearly evident. But through repeated rhythmic swings that ascend ever higher on the evolutionary arc, we will eventually create a society that recognizes and honors the unity and harmony that has always existed just beneath the surface.

NOTES

1. "Marriott Program Helps Low-Wage Workers Cope," *BSR Update: A Publication of Business for Social Responsibility*, August–September 1996, p. 1.

2. "Dow Sets Aggressive Environmental, Health & Safety Goals for 2005: Invests $1 Billion over Next 10 Years," Dow Chemical Company Press Release, 26 April 1996.

3. "The Gospel According to Dr. Mark," *Business Week*, 19 May 1997, p. 61.

4. Rhona Rapoport and Lotte Bailyn. *Relinking Life and Work: Toward a Better Future* (New York: The Ford Foundation, 1996), p. 1.

5. Robert H. Rosen. "The Anatomy of a Healthy Company," in *New Traditions in Business: Spirit and Leadership in the 21st Century*, ed. John Renesch (San Francisco: Berrett-Koehler Publishers, 1992), p. 115.

6. Wilber, p. 225.

7. Ibid, pp. 229–231.

8. Ibid, p. 260.

9. Dana Milbank, Valerie Reitman, Dianne Solis, and Paulette Thomas. "Women in Business: A Global Report Card," *Wall Street Journal*, 26 July 1995, p. 1(B).

10. David Woodruff. "Women Lead the Pack in East German Startups," *Business Week*, 6 June 1996, p. 26.

11. Judy Wicks. "Women Changing Business," *Philadelphia Inquirer*, 6 March 1995, p. 5(E).

12. *Women: The New Providers*, p. 15.

13. Ibid, p. 86.

14. Carol R. Frenier. *Business and The Feminine Principle: The Untapped Resource* (Boston: Butterworth–Heinemann, 1997), p. 105.

15. Wilber, p. 229.

16. June Singer. *Androgyny: Toward a New Theory of Sexuality* (Garden City, NY: Anchor Press/Doubleday, 1976), p. 330.

17. Del Jones. "Companies Won't Derail Diversity," *USA TODAY*, 15 May 1995, p. 1(B).

18. Michele Galen, with Ann Therese Palmer. "Diversity: Beyond the Numbers Game," *Business Week*, 24 August 1995, p. 60.

19. Sanford, p. 203.

20. GTE Corporation. *1994 Annual Report* (Stamford, CT), p. 23.

21. Bob Filipczak. "25 Years of Diversity at UPS," *Training Magazine*, August 1992, p. 2.

22. Ibid, p. 5.

23. Valerie Harms. *The National Audubon Society Almanac of the Environment: The Ecology of Everyday Life* (New York: G.P. Putnam's Sons, 1994), p. 224.

24. John J. Fried. "Firms Take into Account Pollution Practices," *Philadelphia Inquirer*, 20 February 1995, p. 4(E).

25. Minnesota Mining and Manufacturing Company. *Pollution Prevention Pays: Moving Toward Environmental Sustainability*, (St Paul, MN: May 1997), p. 2.

26. "How Nonprofits Help Companies Mind their Waste," *BSR Update: A Publication of Business for Social Responsibility*, June 1996, p. 1.

27. Naisbitt, p. 224.

28. Polaroid Corporation. *Report on the Environment-1993* (Cambridge, MA), p. 3.

29. Ibid, p. 1.

30. "The Superfund Albatross," *Investor's Business Daily*, 23 April 1996, p. 1(B).

31. Timothy Lynch. *Polluting our Principles: Environmental Prosecutions and The Bill of Rights*, Policy Analysis 223 (Washington: The Cato Institute, 1995), p. 5.

32. Del Jones. "Companies Have to Do a Balancing Act," *USA TODAY*, 15 May 1995, p. 2(B).

33. Kenneth H. Blanchard. "Ethics in American Business" in *New Traditions in Business: Spirit and Leadership in the 21st Century*, ed. John Renesch (San Francisco: Berrett-Koehler Publishers, 1992), p. 228.

8

Equilibrium in the New Millennium

A review of the evolution of humanity, from the stone age to the present, reveals periods during which different aspects of our being—physical, social, intellectual and spiritual—take precedence. We are not what we were, nor what we can become. Anthropologists, sociologists and psychologists have studied specific facets of human development, but a unified understanding has been lacking. Spiritual evolution, which deals with the development of consciousness, has received much less attention. Yet it has the unique capacity to clarify all other areas of study, not the least of which is economics and its offspring, commerce.

Just as humanity's level of development affects the institutions and enterprises through which it functions, so too is humanity affected by the policies and practices of these organizations. It has been shown that more caring and enlightened citizens are beginning to have a positive impact on the businesses that employ them. Dramatic adjustments are occurring in the size and composition of the workforce as well as how corporations reevaluate societal obligations. Because these changes can have a significant impact on our spiritual progress, this chapter will concentrate on the issue of corporate restructuring and its ramifications.

CHANGE IS THE ONLY CONSTANT

Observers of the business scene are well aware that all companies face intense global competition and, as a result, are forced to become more cost- and productivity-conscious. Businesses worldwide are anxious to speed the transition from human workers to less costly forms of artificial intelligence such as robots and computers. Smart machines and networks linking computing and communications are putting a wide array of occupations at risk. From clerks and unskilled laborers to engineers and bank tellers, few workers are likely to be spared. While the transition from people to machines has been going on for several decades, it is only recently that technology has enabled corporations to eliminate layers of middle management, compress job categories, streamline administrative functions and shorten and simplify production and distribution processes. Downsizing and restructuring, with their unpredictable and seemingly capricious layoffs and forced retirements, have resulted in a workplace where worker loyalty and motivation are understandably shaken. Such a volatile climate has generated a high degree of counterproductive stress and resentment.

More progressive managements have tried to counteract this situation by introducing a number of nontraditional perquisites such as time off for employees to care for parents and greater latitude and benefits for those needing to work from home and/or on a part-time basis. They have also begun to delegate greater authority to all levels of the organization. Nonetheless, the reality is that a significant number of people have been unwittingly left with time on their hands. Some predict that corporate re-engineering could eliminate over one million jobs a year for the foreseeable future.[1] In fact, a growing number of businesses are expressing concern about the future consequences of the high-tech revolution.

Percy Barnevik is the former chief executive officer of Asea Brown Boveri (ABB) the multibillion dollar Swiss-Swedish builder of generators and transportation equipment and one of the largest engineering firms in the world. ABB has been a re-engineering participant, cutting around fifty thousand jobs from its payroll the past decade. Barnevik predicts that the proportion of Europe's labor force working in manufacturing and business services will fall from 35 percent to 25 percent in ten years with another decline to 15 percent twenty years down the road. He further states:

> If anybody tells me, wait two or three years and there will be a hell of a demand for labor, I say tell me where? What jobs? In what cities? Which companies? When I add it all together, I find a clear risk that the 10% unemployed or underemployed today could easily become 20 to 25%.[2]

Michael Hammer, former MIT professor and co-author of *Re-engineering the Corporation,* also believes that restructuring is going to have an adverse effect on jobs in the next several decades. "I don't think that we've come close, in fact, to squeezing out what's available to be squeezed," says Hammer.[3]

An alternative to layoffs is to reduce the full-time staff and replace them with part-time workers. This allows employment levels to be adjusted quickly in response to gyrating market conditions. In recent years, BankAmerica Corporation announced that it was turning twelve hundred full-time jobs into part-time employment. More significantly, the bank estimates that less than 20 percent of its employees will be full-time in the future; in fact, nearly six out of ten employees at BankAmerica will work less than twenty hours a week.[4]

Service jobs provide most of the employment opportunities in a mature economy. Since new information networks enable companies to reduce service employment, the consensus view that technology will create more jobs than it destroys is thrown into a state of confusion. Many economists believe that the adverse effects of automation are transitory, but a growing number of forecasters think the current wave of technological change differs from previous ones in several respects. First, no other industrial revolution has been able to affect so many unrelated industries or skill levels. Second, the power of the technology is increasing at an almost exponential rate. The price/performance ratio of computers and related equipment (the combination of prices declining and performance improving) increases at a startling pace, doubling about every eighteen months.[5] This allows even more industries to participate in the technological revolution which, in turn, puts more jobs in jeopardy.

An example of automation affecting even skilled technicians can be found at Pacific Gas & Electric, one of the country's largest utilities. Hundreds of fifty-thousand-dollar-a-year estimators are threatened by a computer program that designs new electric service and estimates installation costs. These new programs make it possible to complete the electrical design of a one-hundred-lot housing development in half an hour versus the one hundred hours it now takes a human technician. PG&E forecasts it will cut its force of five hundred estimators by one-third.[6]

There can be little doubt that we are entering a period where machines increasingly replace human beings. The extent of this trend is illustrated by those who foresee the day when machines will become so proficient at dealing with complexity that they will be able to deal with their own complexity; in essence, machines that can evolve.[7] The ultimate outcome of the struggle between job destruction and job creation may not be known for some time but, at a minimum, it is causing many unsettling short-term repercussions and producing a great deal of consternation for a wide cross section of the labor force.

Sharing the Bounty

What do these developments, which require revisiting the concept of full employment and the sanctity of the work ethic, portend for our social structure? Individuals in most cultures today define themselves in relation to their work. From early childhood, youngsters are continually questioned about what they would like to be when they grow up. After a few short years in a career most people think of themselves primarily as a doctor, lawyer or car mechanic. Consequently, during periods of unemployment or underemployment, self-esteem often plummets. Jeremy Rifkin, author of *The End of Work*, has a number of thoughts on the subject:

> We are being swept up into a powerful new technology revolution that offers the promise of a great transformation, unlike any in history. The new high-technology revolution could mean fewer hours of work and greater benefits for millions. For the first time in modern history, large numbers of human beings could be liberated from long hours of labor in the formal marketplace, to be free to pursue leisure-time activities. The same technological forces could, however, as easily lead to growing unemployment and a global depression. Whether a utopian or dystopian future awaits us depends, to a great measure, on how the productivity gains of the Information Age are distributed.[8]

He goes on to postulate that a fair and equitable distribution of the productivity gains would result in the shortening of the work week around the world. While a commendable goal, the reality is that today's high employment costs (wages, benefits, training and taxes) motivate a company to increase overtime rather than spreading the work around by adding to the workforce. French, British and German employees all have shorter working hours than their counterparts in the U.S., but with higher minimum wages, payroll taxes and mandated benefits, unemployment rates on the continent have been more than double the rates in America.[9]

Surveys show that, when corporations do restructure, management often insists that output remain constant, or even increase, despite fewer workers. In addition, there is frequently a failure to delegate sufficient authority to lower-level employees whose responsibilities have increased due to the contraction of management levels above them. Morale amongst the remaining employees falls leading to increased turnover and, ultimately, lower productivity. Thus, the hoped-for benefits of restructuring may not materialize. In fact, the American Management Association found, in a survey of 1000 companies, that fewer than half the companies undergoing downsizing were actually able to increase their operating profits.

Nitin Nohria, an associate professor at the Harvard Business School, studied layoffs at one hundred large American companies over more than a decade. He found that downsizing generally doesn't pay.[10] Often an excessive number of people are fired or else the wrong ones are let go and those who remain are not retrained to pick up the slack. AT&T announced plans to lay off 40,000 workers in 1996. When it found that it needed to rehire 6,000 workers in certain rapidly growing parts of its business, many of its highly trained employees had already set up their own consulting practices or had begun to work for competing firms.[11] Carrie R. Leana, professor of business administration at the University of Pittsburgh, is unequivocal in her denouncement of today's downsizing:

> The fundamental problem with corporate restructuring as it is practiced today—as an ongoing strategy even in profitable times, rather than as an emergency move—is that it is based on a flawed vision of what makes people and organizations work well. . . . To begin with, it fosters narrow, short-term thinking. . . . In such a culture, who is going to look out for the long-term good of the firm?[12]

Despite the many detractors of downsizing, the business community has long operated on the assumption that it is absolutely necessary to have periodic reductions in force to revitalize their enterprises. Hermes has always held that destruction (restructuring in today's parlance) is a natural and necessary part of the evolutionary process. Because a market economy is dynamic, old outmoded structures and ideas must be continually replaced with newer, more effective ones. In spite of massive layoffs in the U.S. over the past decade, considerably more jobs have been created than destroyed. In Europe, where laws and customs make it much harder to reduce the workforce, unemployment rates have remained much higher and the overall economy has languished. When corporate layoffs and restructurings are implemented with deliberation and compassion they will not only increase productivity but win the indispensable support of the surrounding community. Case in point: Levi Strauss & Co. announced the closing, in 1998, of eleven of their U.S. facilities as a consequence of rising competition resulting in decreased demand for their denim products. Close to 6400 employees lost their jobs as a result. This is hardly the kind of action any company wants to take, especially one with a stellar reputation for treating its workers fairly. But the company negotiated a severance package with the union that far exceeded industry standards and showed a heartfelt concern for the welfare of those affected. In addition to the usual severance provisions, the company added a number of unusually generous benefits:

- Three weeks pay for each year of service plus eight months notice pay.
- Continuation of health care benefits for up to 18 months.
- A $500 bonus paid upon securing new employment.
- A $6,000 allowance for such things as relocation, education and retraining, dependent care and business startup expenses, chosen at the employees' option.
- Eligible employees will receive a full payout of the previously announced 2002 profit-sharing plan assuming the company meets their publicly stated financial objectives.

In addition, the Levi Strauss Foundation designated $8 million in grants to help nonprofit organizations in communities hurt by the plant closings.

It appears that the company thought long and hard before taking these steps and put together a package that will make the dislocation as painless as possible. But perhaps the most unusual aspect is their willingness to share the benefits of expense reductions with these former employees despite the fact that they will not be working for the company in 2002 when the profit sharing is due to be allocated.[13]

In general, however, recent business cutbacks may have been larger than necessary and the gains derived from the introduction of new technology have been retained almost exclusively by the stockholders and management in the form of higher dividends and larger executive compensation. Workers' claims on productivity advances are often seen to be of tertiary importance compared to those who contribute the capital and oversee the operations.

In the long run, of course, this is a shortsighted, win/lose attitude. Although a majority of the productivity gains might initially accrue to the owners, if they are not shared within a reasonable period of time, morale and motivation will suffer and the benefits will increasingly dissipate. In this rapidly changing and fiercely competitive business environment, a skilled, creative and dedicated workforce is essential. In the past, when diversity and environmental issues were neglected by business, they paid a price. A similar undesirable outcome can be expected unless business ceases its myopic practice of hoarding all productivity increases for itself. Jeremy Rifkin foresees the possibility of an optimistic resolution:

> There is reason to be hopeful that a new vision based on transformation of consciousness and a new commitment to community will take hold. With millions of human beings spending more and more of their waking hours away from work in the formal economy, in the years ahead the importance of formal work to their lives will diminish as well—including its hold over their concept of self-worth. The diminution of work life in the formal economy is going to mean decreased allegiance to the values, world view, and vision that accompany the marketplace. If an alternative vision steeped in the ethos of personal transformation, community restoration, and environmental consciousness were to gain widespread currency, the intellectual foundation could be laid for the post-market era.[14]

When productivity gains are equitably distributed, history shows that, all things being equal, they are likely to result in a shorter work week. In the case of the first two industrial revolutions, which covered the period from the early 1800s through World War I, the question of rising unemployment for some versus greater leisure for many was finally settled in favor of the latter. There was, however, a protracted battle between labor and management before the issue was resolved. In the nineteenth century, productivity gains resulted in a reduction in the number of hours worked per week from eighty to sixty.

Likewise, in the early part of the twentieth century, as we went from steam to oil and electric power, productivity increases enabled businesses to reduce the time spent at work from sixty to forty hours per week. As we move into and through the information revolution, a growing number of observers believe that time on the job can again be reduced to between twenty and thirty hours per week. Those who are skeptical of this possibility should note that, despite a doubling of American productivity since 1948 (we can now produce our 1948 standard of living in less than half the time it took in that year), United States workers are working longer hours today than several decades ago.[15] The U.S. Labor Department survey of households shows that the average worker spent 39.2 hours per week on the job in 1996 versus 37.7 in 1982.[16] And compared to their counterparts overseas, U.S. workers get minimal vacations. Runzheimer International reported that the average American worker gets less than half as much time off as do employees in much of Europe and Japan.[17] Even if future technological advances are ignored, there would clearly be room to shorten the work week. Accomplished in an equitable manner, this could help alleviate future employment problems.

What Is Your Leisure?

There is considerable historical precedent for spending less time being gainfully employed. Throughout the world, today's workers spend more time working than did those of many ancient societies. The Egyptians proscribed work for about seventy days a year, about one day out of every five. The Romans of the fourth century had 175 holidays. In Tsarist Russia, there were over a hundred religious holidays every year, while in some parts of Galicia the number of non-working days was reported to have exceeded two hundred. The Hopi Indians of the southwestern United States reserved more than half the year for leisure activities. And finally, some of the Greek city-states had more than one hundred and eighty days away from work.[18] Interestingly, the Greek concept of *paideia*—a society in which learning, fulfillment and becoming fully human are the primary goals to which all institutions are directed—is ideally suited to time away from formal work. According to Werner Jaeger, the foremost scholar of *paideia*, its central theme was the individual's "search for the Divine Center."[19] This would certainly be a worthy pursuit for a society that is increasing its ability to maintain a high standard of living while spending less time on the job. As suggested by the late Willis Harman:

> In a technologically advanced society where production of sufficient goods and services can be handled with ease, *employment exists primarily for self-development, and is only secondarily concerned with the production of goods and services.* This concept of work represents a profound shift in our perceptions with implications that reverberate throughout the entire structure of industrial society.[20]

While there is still some guilt attached to not working, perhaps because of a nagging feeling that our free time should be devoted to a higher purpose than having fun, interest in the shorter work week has been spreading from labor leaders and policy analysts to the general public. A survey conducted by the Families and Work Institute showed that a significant number of Americans would accept some reduction in income for more leisure time. Workers say they want to spend more time and energy on their personal lives even at the expense of career advancement.[21] A corroborating survey, released by Robert Half

International Inc., revealed that nearly two-thirds of Americans would reduce their hours and compensation in exchange for more personal and family time. On average they would be willing to accept a 21 percent reduction in pay to obtain more flexibility. This is a 50 percent increase over results from a similar survey taken just seven years earlier.[22] These desires echo the Aristotelian view that the goal of life is happiness and that leisure, as distinguished from amusement or recreation, is a prerequisite for its achievement.[23] A more contemporary spokesperson, Yoneji Masuda, a key architect of Japan's computer advancements, envisions a future where free time eclipses material accumulation as the primary goal of society. Indeed, Masuda considers this emerging paradigm to be a turning point in the evolution of our species.[24]

But what should we do with our free time? One alternative is community service. This "work" encompasses everything from rebuilding our neighborhoods, both physically and morally, to ministering to the needs and aspirations of the millions of individuals who, for various reasons, are suffering ill health or living in poverty. Community service is driven by an appreciation that all things are interconnected and is motivated by a desire to give something back to society. While a large number of individuals have the wherewithal to forgo any remuneration for their effort, many of the newly unemployed may need financial assistance. Corporations that are reaping the benefits of technological productivity increases may be persuaded to support some of the unemployed who work for causes they find most worthy. Without a safe, clean and prosperous community, material success is both fleeting and unsatisfying.

In addition, the elimination of "corporate welfare" that, in most cases, can no longer be economically justified, could free up billions of dollars. According to the Cato Institute, the federal government spends more than $75 billion a year on more than 125 programs that provide direct taxpayer assistance to U.S. businesses.[25] Corporate welfare includes direct government grants, loans, insurance, or subsidies provided to business; trade barriers designed to protect specific firms from foreign competition at the expense of the United States consumer; and loopholes in the tax code that have the specific purpose of benefiting a particular company or industry. Corporate giveaways divert the industrialists' attention from the marketplace to the political arena. They thereby give politically connected firms an unfair advantage and distort the efficient allocation of resources. This situation also creates a bidding war for preferential treatment among businesses and industries. Farm subsidies, such as the Market Promotion Program, fund foreign advertising for financially healthy corporations such as General Mills Inc., M&M/Mars, Sunkist Growers Inc. and McDonald's Corporation. McDonald's, for instance, received $200,000 to help advertise Chicken McNuggets in Singapore.[26]

Many weapons programs are likewise welfare for corporations. Weapons are often purchased, not because they are needed for the nation's security, but because the spending "creates jobs" or helps a politician in his home district. Not only are these handouts inappropriate given both a huge national debt and the end of the cold war, but they usually fail to accomplish their intended purpose. Benefits received by one group are offset by losses elsewhere in the economy. Robert Shapiro, of the Progressive Policy Institute, points out that subsidies artificially raise an industry's rate of return, shielding it from normal competitive forces thereby enabling it to put off improving its product or lowering its prices. These entitlements also make taxpayers/consumers transfer more resources to these favored sectors than would otherwise be the case.[27] Since it is not likely this corporate largesse will be eliminated in the near future, corporations have a heightened obligation to help those who are volunteering their time or to aid those whose income has fallen below some predetermined level.

Much more could be said about the relationship between voluntary community service and the availability of leisure time. As commendable and satisfying as service projects are, however, they are, like experiences at work, usually outer-directed. A preponderance of our time is currently spent on activities that keep attention focused in an outward direction. Exclusive attention to such experiences prevents us from reaching the high levels of self-actualization and fulfillment that we all seek and are capable of achieving. One purpose of this book, therefore, is to bring attention to the need for inner work. For if we are to realize our highest aspirations, we will need to bring the time spent on inner and outer work into better balance.

Humanity's deep-seated desire for a balanced life is confirmed in a survey prepared by The Harwood Group, a public issues research firm in Bethesda, Maryland. The study was commissioned by the Merck Family Fund to provide a statistical picture of how Americans view issues connected to consumption, the environment and the values and priorities held by contemporary society. A key finding to emerge from the survey was that "Americans believe our priorities are out of whack."[28] They feel materialism, greed, and selfishness increasingly eclipse a more meaningful set of values centered on family, responsibility and community. More specifically:

> People express a strong desire for a greater sense of **balance** (emphasis added) in their lives—not to repudiate material gain, but to bring it more into proportion with the non-material rewards of life. . . . They see their fellow Americans growing increasingly atomized, selfish and irresponsible; they worry that our society is losing its moral center. They believe our priorities are mixed up.[29]

Many participants believed that excessive materialism is at the root of many of our social problems, such as crime and drugs. "Things have become so important to us that things and the acquisition of things run our lives and our relations with others."[30] In the study, 82 percent felt that most people buy and consume far more than they need. And 93 percent stated that an underlying cause of environmental problems is that Americans' lifestyle produces too much waste. The research suggested that people truly aspire to live in harmony with their values. As stated in the report, "People seem to yearn for things money cannot buy: more time, less stress, a sense of balance."[31] In fact, 67 percent agreed with the statement, "I would like to have more balance in my life."[32] They believe that the essential functions of life which center around family, friends and community have been shoved aside by the pressure for "more, more, more," and they want to restore a greater sense of stability.[33]

In fact, despite an extensive social safety net to help assuage our guilt about the poor and disadvantaged and the widespread availability of ostentatious luxuries for the rich and famous, a large portion of humanity is dissatisfied with their plight. A special seventy-fifth anniversary issue of *Forbes* magazine asked eleven of our most prominent writers and scholars to ponder the question, "Why do Americans feel so bad when they've got it so good?" Or, as the editor of *Forbes* wrote in an introduction to the last of the contributors, "As we stand here in 1992, just eight years short of the beginning of the Third Millennium A.D., we sense throughout the world a bewildering juxtaposition of material progress and spiritual discontent. What does it mean, this angst?"[34] The answers were quite varied and generally unsatisfying. Based on the material covered in the previous chapters, the answer seems rather obvious; having all the "things" in the world will not give us what we truly want. Ultimate peace and contentment can only be achieved by making contact with the essence of our being. Alfred Kazin, one of America's most distinguished men of letters, commenting on the problem in *Forbes* said, "And the malaise is even more cultural and spiritual than it is economic."[35] Author Peter Russell puts our feelings of discontent in an historical/spiritual context:

> There is a shift in our societies to begin to look inwardly. I think it's very parallel to what the Buddha went through, two and a half thousand years ago. He had all the riches one could want but it didn't end suffering, so he went out on his search to find a different way. That is happening en masse in our society to millions and millions of people who are beginning to look for something new.[36]

EASTSIDE, WESTSIDE

An interesting convergence of two cultures is taking place; one that may provide for what is lacking in each. While the West is well known for its material successes and scientific achievements, the East is generally regarded as less advanced technologically but replete with mystical holy men and enriching spiritual practices. While both cultures are moving toward a more balanced mixture of inner and outer work, each may have much to learn by studying the other's traditions and priorities. This would certainly be in accord with Hermes' deepest longings—the attainment of a union between reason and inspiration, science and religion.[37]

Hinduism, generally regarded as the oldest living religion, has no founder or uniform dogma. Its scriptures and seers teach that all creatures are in a process of spiritual evolution that proceeds through an untold number of cycles. BRAHMAN, the non-personal SUPREME ONE, both pervades and transcends all things. Humans are able, through personal effort, to use inner knowledge and consciously unite with THE CREATOR while still incarnate. While most of its more than five hundred million followers live in India, adherents can be found in Africa, the Pacific Islands and many parts of the West. Hindu scriptures proclaim that a normal, harmonious life consists of four stages. First, a youth begins a course of study and service. This is followed by marriage and duty to family and community.[38] Upon reaching the third stage (between forty and fifty years of life), the Hindu detaches himself from materialistic and family obligations and turns towards a life of contemplation and gradual withdrawal from worldly ties. In other words, he begins the process of "letting go," or what we might call retirement. The sons may take over the business as the elders move away from family connections and societal ties, and seek the inner strength to go on to the fourth stage where the ultimate goal is to experience union with the soul.[39]

While Hindu religious beliefs, such as the unity of all things, once seemed alien to the western mind, much of its wisdom has been authenticated by modern science. Might western man also find that, by following a similar four-stage pattern over the course of his life, he is better able to attain the peace and happiness that has too often eluded him? It is in stage three, in particular, that the East and West part company. For most individuals in our culture, the time between forty and fifty is the peak of their career growth. The external world beckons with the opportunity to earn ever-greater amounts of money which can be used to acquire more possessions. But, as we have seen, additional possessions cannot be equated with peace and fulfillment.

Could it be that, once our children are raised and other obligations taken care of, we are best served by a life that emphasizes contemplation and study rather accumulating more of the material goods that are required during the first four or five decades of life? This "stage of life" concept may be accorded greater credence based on the fact that other spiritual traditions espouse much the same idea. The Kabbalah, the mystical teachings of Judaism, discourages aspirants from seeking instruction until they have raised their families and mastered the rudiments of physical survival. Then, sometime after reaching forty years of age, a concentrated period of study and meditation is encouraged. Although many people express surprise that the Jewish tradition contains a meditative system that is similar to that of the East, this resemblance was first noted in the Zohar, the most famous of Kabbalistic writings. The promulgation of meditation in these different systems can be seen as a reflection of the efficacy of this technique for releasing oneself from the illusion of separation and the exclusive identification with physicality.[40]

THERE ARE NO MISTAKES

What, it might be asked, does spiritual training and ritual have to do with the changes taking place in the business world? Could the fact that civilization has evolved to the point where material needs are met with less time and effort than ever before, be an important message? Are we being prodded to reorder our priorities and reallocate our time? Put another way, the universe seems to be presenting us with the opportunity to devote less time to external sense and security issues and direct more of our energy toward becoming receptive to internal experiences and influences. Sacred writings from all traditions maintain that such experiences are open to all sincere seekers.

It makes little difference that this idea of universal intercession may seem too improbable to gain wide acceptance; the reason events unfold as they do is not important. The fact remains that, in little over a century, we have dramatically reduced the number of hours we need to work to meet our daily needs. It is paramount, therefore, that we take advantage of this opportunity and use our increasing leisure time to seek our hearts' desire; union with that which transcends the material aspects of life. Returning to Vaclav Havel's 1994 Independence Day speech:

> Only someone who submits to the authority of the universal order and of creation, who values the right to be a part of it and a participant in it, can genuinely value himself and his neighbors, and thus honor their rights as well. . . . The truly reliable path to coexistence . . . and creative cooperation, must start from what is at the root of all cultures and what lies infinitely deeper in human hearts and minds. . . . It must be rooted in self-transcendence. . . . Transcendence as a deeply and joyously experienced need to be in harmony even with what we ourselves are not, what we do not understand, what seems distant from us in time and space, but with which we are nevertheless mysteriously linked because, together with us, all this constitutes a single world. Transcendence [is] the only real alternative to extinction.[41]

How can we accelerate our connection to that which is higher?

GO MEDITATE ON IT

While meditative techniques vary from culture to culture, they have almost always been developed by individuals referred to as mystics. The root of the word "mystic" is the same as that of the word "close." The mystic's goal is to close off all artificial influences that prevent knowing one's true nature.[42] The senses merely reflect the illusory world of separation rather than ultimate reality wherein all individual threads are actually part of one tapestry. When the misery that inevitably arises from being bound to surface appearances and temporal sensations becomes intolerable, such as when we are afflicted with disease, we are forced to find a way to alleviate our pain. By first concentrating on the problem, then contemplating alternative ways of thinking and behaving and finally meditating and praying, we make ourselves receptive to guidance from our divine center. Since the solution to any problem is always available if we possess a sufficiently intense desire and exercise a great deal of patience, we will eventually be able to rediscover that which we once knew but lost.

Ageless wisdom tells us that most scientific advances come about through a process of rediscovery as opposed to the unearthing of new information. This recollection process may be thought of as gaining access to that which was forgotten during the involutionary journey. By grasping the fact that we are intimately connected to the universe and have access to every part of its consciousness, we become increasingly able to absorb more of its infinite wisdom. Such an understanding resolves all fears and anxieties and provides the power to heal disease and dissolve discomfort. The commentary of Swami Prabhavananda on the aphorisms of the great Indian sage Patanjali, helps clarify the process and goal of meditation:

> Beginning at the surface of life, the meditative mind goes inward, seeking always the cause behind the appearance, and then the cause behind the cause, until the innermost Reality is reached.[43]

Mystics from every religious/spiritual persuasion—Zen, Sufi, Christian, Hindu, Jewish, etc.—have a different view of reality than that ordinarily observed. This is not to say that the more common, everyday view is wrong; it simply means that there are at least two ways of comprehending reality. The illusion of separation is necessary for the evolution of self-consciousness but we must guard against becoming deluded into thinking that the images we derive from our senses are the most accurate or the only picture of life. On one level, the more commonly accepted view works better while, on a different level, another is more effective. A mystic, who may have achieved a state in which he experiences the mental substance that underlies and forms all matter, will likely operate more effectively in his daily activities if he treats the walls of a room as if they were the solid material they appear to be. He knows the reality that lies below the surface but, from an everyday, pragmatic standpoint, it is best to obey the laws of the physical plane. In physics there is a concept known as the principle of complementarity. It states that, for the most comprehensive understanding of some phenomena, we need two different points of view. The mystic also claims that, to reach one's highest potential, a person needs these two viewpoints. This second way of perceiving, wherein life is seen holistically and all appearances of separation are unified, is the heart of the meditative state.[44]

There is nothing arcane or unusual about meditation. From the conservative American Medical Association to buttoned-down corporations, meditation is being used for everything from decreasing high blood pressure to increasing productivity. Herbert Benson, Harvard Medical School professor and author of a book on meditation, receives approximately half a dozen calls a week from HMOs inquiring about emerging research that health care use is lower among those who pray or meditate.[45] Programs presented by respected commentators such as Bill Moyers and Dr. Dean Ornish have also extolled the benefits of meditational practices. What is being discovered is that, just as the body transcends matter and the intellect transcends the body, in meditation the soul transcends the intellect. How important is it to transcend the intellect through meditational practices? According to Ken Wilber:

And, if we—you and I—are to further the evolution of mankind, and not just reap the benefit of past humanity's struggles, if we are to contribute to evolution and not merely siphon it off, if we are to help the overcoming of our self-alienation from spirit and not merely perpetuate it, then meditation—or a similar and truly contemplative practice—becomes an absolute ethical imperative, a new categorical imperative. If we do less than that, our life then becomes, not so much a wicked affair, but rather a case of merely enjoying the level of conscience which past heroes achieved for us. We contribute nothing; we pass on our mediocrity.[46]

RETURNING TO WHERE WE STARTED

The evolutionary path spirals round and round, each turn higher than the preceding one. Based on the observations made in previous chapters, humanity has made considerable progress and there is much to look forward to in the years ahead. Transformative changes that are unfolding now or can be expected as we move into the third millennium include:

- Humanity transcends all roles based on characteristics such as gender, color and race as the globalization of work and leisure activities enables us to focus on commonly shared aspirations rather than dwelling on apparent differences.
- Both personal and organizational decisions will be based, with an ever-greater degree of confidence, on our intuitional faculties as we realize there is much more to life than what we can receive from our physical senses.
- Economic priorities are adjusted to reflect a world of realizable abundance rather than apparent scarcity. This results in a willingness by businesses to place ethical values and social responsibility ahead of short-term profitability and win/lose strategies.
- Education increasingly becomes a lifetime activity the ultimate aim of which is self-knowledge which leads to a

greater appreciation of self-worth. Learning institutions minimize the memorization of facts and focus instead on a comprehensive understanding of the relationship among, and relative importance of, body, mind and spirit.

- Technological advances are used to enable humanity to spend more time on its inner work as there is growing acceptance that it is this aspect of life that will bring an ultimate sense of peace and fulfillment.[47]
- Prosperity will be redefined to encompass much more than external power or material wealth. These traditional measures of success will be considered desirable only to the extent they also foster ethically, morally and spiritually sensitive human beings whose primary motivation is to develop long-term, sustainable and caring relationships with all of the other inhabitants of the planet.
- Socially responsible investing (SRI) becomes the norm rather than the exception. More specifically, investors place increasing weight on SRI screening as evidence mounts that these filters provide the best gauge for determining the overall quality of a company's management by identifying those with superior employee and customer relations.

Early in the book, the seven Hermetic Principles were described in detail. These Principles undoubtedly challenged the belief system of many readers as what they purport goes beyond what most individuals have personally experienced. The intellect is understandably reluctant to accept what cannot be known through the senses. As we continue our journey, deepening our inner work, ageless wisdom assures us that a higher level of reality will unfold in concert with expanded self-consciousness. The founders of the world's major religions have told us, both indirectly through parables and directly in scriptures that, in time, it becomes possible to experience personally the mental substance which forms all physical manifestations. Humankind will come to know the hierarchical structure of the universe with its ascending vibrational levels and with the mirror-like correspondences that exist among the various levels. We will be able to understand the causes that lie behind all effects and the unity that lies behind all pairs of opposites. We will see the underlying rhythm that swings us from pole to pole as we learn our lessons. And we will move ever closer to a balanced, androgynous state, as we comprehend that there is really only "one thing" and that "one thing" contains all things within itself. As humanity evolves it will be ever closer to living in harmony with the way things were before the involutional journey began and the way life is destined to be once the evolutionary passage has been completed.

The introduction to this book began with several quotations. Vaclav Havel described the confusing, often chaotic times we live in, while Anita Roddick spoke to the need for a new framework for business so it can be a force for social change. Chaos and upheaval bring the opportunity and the responsibility for breakthroughs to new understandings. As described throughout this book, the business community is now on the cutting edge of a paradigm shift. Once an ethic based on wholeness (cooperation and cocreation), compassion (caring and sharing) and benevolence (access to all the body needs and the heart desires) is fully embraced—as one based on the seven Hermetic Principles is obliged to do—businesses worldwide will have the opportunity to lead humanity to heights heretofore unimagined.

For the concluding chapter, in-depth personal interviews and extended field trips were undertaken to gain a comprehensive understanding of two companies with rich histories of value-driven leadership. While perhaps not recognized explicitly, the seven Hermetic Principles are evident in the conduct of the everyday practices of these two businesses. A greater acceptance and appreciation for the practicality of this ancient wisdom may be realized as we study the policies and activities of these two companies.

NOTES

1. Jeremy Rifkin. *The End of Work: The Decline of the Global Labor Force and the Dawn of the Post-Market Era* (New York: Jeremy P. Tarcher/Putnam Books, 1995), p. 7.

2. "Apocalypse—But Not Just Now," *Financial Times,* 4 January 1993, p. 30.

3. Rifkin, quoting his interview with Michael Hammer, 6 May 1994, p. 103.

4. Ibid, 190.

5. Pascal G. Zachary. "Worried Workers," *Wall Street Journal,* 8 June 1995, p. 1(A).

6. Ibid.

7. Rifkin, p. 61.

8. Ibid, p. 13.

9. "Share the Work," *Investor's Business Daily,* 6 June 1997, p. 1(B).

10. David E. Sanger and Steve Lohr. "The Downsizing of America, Is There a Better Way? A Search for Answers," *New York Times,* 9 March 1996, p. 10.

11. Paul Sperry. "Corporate Bulimia," *Investor's Business Daily,* 9 April 1996, p. 4(A).

12. Carrie R. Leana. "Why Downsizing Is Bad for Business," *Philadelphia Inquirer,* 5 January 1996, p. 15(A).

13. "Levi Strauss & Co. Announces Plant Closure Plans in the U.S.," San Francisco, CA, 3 November 1997; available from http://www.levistrauss.com; accessed November 10, 1997.

14. Rifkin, p. 247.

15. Ibid, pp. 222–3.

16. Gene Koretz. "How Many Hours in a Workweek?" *Business Week,* 16 June 1997, p. 28.

17. Gene Koretz. "Yankees: Nose to the Grindstone," *Business Week,* 4 September 1995, p. 28.

18. Witold Rybczynski. *Waiting for the Weekend* (New York: Viking Penguin, 1991), pp. 52–53.

19. Harman, p. 129.

20. Ibid, p. 146.

21. Rifkin, p. 233.

22. "Time with Kids More Important than Money," *Investor's Business Daily*, 11 June 1996, p. 4(A).

23. Rybczynski, p. 21.

24. Rifkin, p. 222.

25. Stephen Moore and Dean Stansel. *How Corporate Welfare Won*, Policy Analysis 254 (Washington: The Cato Institute, 1996), p. 1.

26. John Merline. "Corporations at the Trough?" *Investor's Business Daily*, 12 March 1996, p. 1(A).

27. Ibid.

28. *Yearning for Balance*, p. 1.

29. Ibid, p. 3.

30. Ibid, p. 4.

31. Ibid, p. 15.

32. Ibid, p. 16.

33. Ibid, p. 23.

34. John Ashbery. "A Last Word from a Poet," *Forbes*, 14 September 1992, p. 193.

35. Ibid.

36. Peter Russell. "A Shift in Consciousness: Implications for Business," interview by Willis Harman, *World Business Academy Perspectives* 9, no 4 (1995): p. 65.

37. Faivre, p. 105.

38. *Great Religions of the World* (New York: National Geographic Book Service, 1978), pp. 36–37.

39. Stanley Wolpert. *India* (Oxford: University of California Press, 1991), pp. 124–125.

40. Aryeh Kaplan. *Meditation and Kabbalah* (York Beach, ME: Samuel Weiser, 1982), p. 3.

41. Havel, p. 6.

42. Lawrence LeShan. *How to Meditate* (New York: Bantam Books, 1974), p. 7.

43. Swami Prabhavananda and Christopher Isherwood, trans. *How To Know God: The Yogi Aphorisms of Patanjali* (New York: Mentor Books, 1969), p. 28.

44. LeShan, pp. 8, 11.

45. Joseph Pereira. "The Healing Power of Prayer Is Tested By Science," *Wall Street Journal,* 20 December 1995, p. 1(B).

46. Wilber, p. 321.

47. Ibid, p. 325.

9

Tying It All Together—
A Tale of Two Companies

The transformative thinking being embraced by leaders through-out the industrialized world has been described in the last several chapters. Businesses have begun to implement practices which were once considered ivory tower fantasies. Clearly, some of the changes have been defensive in nature and, at least initially, motivated by the expectation of positive publicity. Nonetheless, many companies are making momentous shifts in the way they are structured, in the ordering of their priorities and in the be-havior they exhibit toward their many constituencies. Who are the individuals at the vanguard of these changes? Which companies have made the most progress in integrating holistic thinking with pragmatic policy initiatives? To answer these questions, we began a search for an organization whose membership is motivated by a combination of idealism and pragmatism, and whose agenda is to promote the common good. Such an organization would likely include the type of companies for which we were looking.

The Coalition for Environmentally Responsible Economies (CERES) was formed in 1989 and boasts a membership that includes investors, environmental activists, religious organizations and representatives from the labor movement. Without resorting to confrontational or adversarial action, CERES encourages businesses to become much more attentive to the environment. Since coalition member organizations represent more than ten million people and have over $150 billion in invested assets, they are quite influential and have a significant stake in the financial success of the business community. By forging a relationship of mutual respect and cooperation between the public at large and the corporate world, CERES attempts to develop an atmosphere wherein all parties can claim success.[1] Membership in CERES is neither a seal of approval nor a certification. Those companies that pledge to improve their environmental practices steadily over time and to report each year on their progress deserve commendation for their very visible commitment. More importantly, by becoming signatories, they have courageously agreed to become publicly accountable for a broad range of policies and activities. Businesses endorsing the principles of CERES (see Figure 9–1) pledge to monitor and improve their environmental practices in a number of specifically delineated areas.

Companies of all types and sizes, including a significant number in the Fortune 500, are represented. It seems reasonable to expect that such forward-looking companies will also exhibit heightened sensitivity to the needs of all their stakeholders. From this list of endorsing companies, two were selected. The companies chosen for in-depth analysis have very different operating characteristics, yet both have a long history of bold leadership. They cater to two very basic industries and both corporations face mounting competitive pressures. One is quite small; the other relatively large. One is privately controlled; the other publicly owned. One acknowledges that it has much work to do in the field of pollution abatement while the other is known for its staunch environmental record. As described below, both of these companies have numerous qualities worthy of emulation.

WALNUT ACRES—A BUSINESS AS OLD AS THE HILLS

One of the earliest pioneers to exhibit both innovative and egalitarian leadership was Paul Keene. In 1946, he founded Walnut Acres and introduced a "new" method of farming to America. From very simple beginnings, the company has become the country's largest mail-order organic food producer. This family- and employee-run organization covers all facets of the organic food business including the growing, processing, packaging and distribution of over 350 products. Each year approximately thirty thousand visitors tour a 100,000-square-foot plant that cans sixty containers of soup a minute and a mill that grinds one thousand pounds of whole wheat flour an hour.[2] Despite the use of such modern equipment, the company adheres to traditional organic farming methods based on those of the British agricultural visionary, Sir Albert Howard, who said, "Each generation has the sacred duty to hold over, unimpaired, the heritage of a healthy, fertile soil, [and] always put back more than we take away."[3] It should be instructive to see where this steadfast reverence for mother nature started and how it is expressed in the company's operations.

Planting the Seeds

The philosophy behind Walnut Acres began in India where founder Paul Keene and his wife Betty, now deceased, met and married. Keene's decision to change his career and lifestyle began in the late 1930s. After finishing his graduate work at Yale in 1936, he taught in the mathematics department of Drew University in New Jersey. It was not long before he felt a need to reach beyond what he was doing and he went to India to teach in the missions. While there he was greatly influenced by the Indian people.[4] He felt that they possessed something that was lacking in his life, and was impelled to search for that missing element. They seemed to be able to accommodate themselves to

Figure 9–1 The CERES Principles

By adopting these Principles, we publicly affirm our belief that corporations have a responsibility for the environment, and must conduct all aspects of their business as responsible stewards of the environment by operating in a manner that protects the Earth. We believe that corporations must not compromise the ability of future generations to sustain themselves. We will update our practices constantly in light of advances in technology and new understandings in health and environmental science. In collaboration with CERES, we will promote a dynamic process to ensure that the Principles are interpreted in such a way that accommodates changing technologies and environmental realities. We intend to make consistent, measurable progress in implementing these Principles and to apply them to all aspects of our operations throughout the world.

Protection of the Biosphere

We will reduce and make continual progress toward eliminating the release of any substance that may cause environmental damage to the air, water, the earth or its inhabitants. We will safeguard all habitats affected by our operations and will protect open spaces and wilderness, while preserving biodiversity.

Sustainable Use of Natural Resources

We will make sustainable use of renewable natural resources, such as water, soils and forests. We will conserve nonrenewable natural resources through efficient use and careful planning.

Reduction and Disposal of Wastes

We will reduce and where possible eliminate waste through source reduction and recycling. All waste will be handled and disposed of through safe and responsible methods.

Energy Conservation

We will conserve energy and improve the energy efficiency of our internal operations and of the goods and services we sell. We will make every effort to use environmentally safe and sustainable energy sources.

Risk Reduction

We will strive to minimize the environmental, health and safety risks to our employees and the communities in which we operate through safe technologies, facilities and operating procedures, and by being prepared for emergencies.

Safe Products and Services

We will reduce and where possible eliminate the use, manufacture or sale of products and services that cause environmental damage or health or safety hazards. We will inform our customers of the environmental impacts of our products or services and try to correct unsafe use.

Environmental Restoration

We will promptly and responsibly correct conditions we have caused that endanger health, safety or the environment. To the extent feasible, we will redress injuries we have caused to persons or damage we have caused to the environment and will restore the environment.

Informing the Public

We will inform in a timely manner everyone who may be affected by conditions caused by our company that might endanger health, safety or the environment. We will regularly seek advice and counsel through dialogue with persons in communities near our facilities. We will not take any action against employees for reporting dangerous incidents or conditions to management or appropriate authorities.

Management Commitment

We will implement theses Principles and sustain a process that ensures that the Board of Directors and Chief Executive Officer are fully informed about pertinent environmental issues and are fully responsible for environmental policy. In selecting our Board of Directors we will consider demonstrated environmental commitment as a factor.

Audits and Reports

We will conduct an annual self-evaluation of our progress in implementing these Principles. We will support the timely creation of generally accepted environmental audit procedures. We will annually complete the CERES Report, which will be made available to the public.

Disclaimer

These Principles establish an ethic with criteria by which investors and others can assess the environmental performance of companies. Companies that endorse these Principles pledge to go voluntarily beyond the requirements of the law. The terms may and might in Principles one and eight are not meant to encompass every imaginable consequence, no matter how remote. Rather, these Principles obligate endorsers to behave as prudent persons who are not governed by conflicting interests and who possess a strong commitment to environmental excellence and to human health and safety. These Principles are not intended to create new legal liabilities, expand existing rights or obligations, waive legal defenses, or otherwise affect the legal position of any endorsing company, and are not intended to be used against an endorser in a legal proceeding for any purpose.

The CERES Principles (Boston). Used with permission.

circumstances, believing that life was more than possessions. It could almost be said that in their poverty lay their riches.[5] In India he became part of a delegation of Americans who met to offer support to Mahatma Gandhi and his independence movement. He came to know Gandhi and, along with others, would accompany him on his morning walks.[6] When his planned career no longer held the promise of satisfaction, he began to wonder if he had become too separated from life at its core. In his search for the missing quality in his life, he asked Gandhi how a young person could best serve humanity and the world. He was told, "When you return to your home in America, you must give away everything you have. Don't owe anything. Then you will be free to talk and act. Doors will open for you." Although he did not follow Gandhi's counsel in all respects, he chose a way of life wherein he would be more in touch with the fundamentals of life and more directly dependent on the soil, as were the people of India.[7]

A year after returning to the United States, Keene was sure a career in mathematics did not mesh with his inner desires. With the appeal of the earth beckoning, he and his wife enrolled in an organic farming school. This eventually led to their purchase of a 108-acre farm in the tiny village of Penns Creek, Pennsylvania.[8] In the years that followed, he heeded much of Gandhi's advice as he relinquished his academic profession, gave partial ownership in his company to the employees and started a charitable foundation which enjoys the full support of the company's money and workforce. According to Keene, "Our whole life we have tried to be helpful and think of everybody in this world being a brother and sister of ours. That's hard to live by, but ultimately I think that's the basis of life."[9]

Giving Back

The Walnut Acres Foundation was established in 1960 to provide space and support for those encountering adversity. Operating both locally and internationally, it is involved in community-based activities and life assistance programs. The company donated land for a community center in its hometown of Penns Creek which was, at the time, suffering from the limited economic resources of neighboring Appalachia. The center sponsors activities for residents of all ages and houses a day care center and preschool. The foundation's other beneficiary, Family Village Farms, started in 1969 in South India, provided a tangible outlet for the Keene's deep belief in the unity of all people. This ten-acre plot of land was purchased as an addition to an orphanage and school which is dedicated to teaching life skills to homeless children in accordance with the Gandhian principle of cottage industries. The primary aim of both of these programs is to help children develop fully: physically, mentally and spiritually.

One of the unusual aspects of the foundation is that all donations can go directly to the beneficiaries. This is because Walnut Acres, its employees and volunteers give their time, energy and resources to the running of the Foundation. All salaries, advertising, printing, mailing and overhead expenses are paid for by the company. As Bob Anderson, Keene's son-in-law and President of Walnut Acres, notes, "We wanted to set about showing what business could and should do, and that communities need not be solely dependent on government to provide them with the things they need."[10] How does this philosophy of giving back more than is taken manifest in the company's customer, employee and environmental policies?

Establishing Roots

In the early days, the Keenes had to reverse the then popular practice of extracting every last bit of fertility from the soil and begin the process of adding extra organic matter so the earth could be replenished. Plowing under cash crops was not easy, as their growing family of five had to live sparingly. They were often ostracized for their unconventional practices; they were called communists, threatened with tar and feathers and had a cross burned on their lawn because they were so different.[11] Their deep commitment to treat the earth with utmost respect enabled them to persevere. Keene writes:

> Our whole emphasis has been on treating the soil as the living entity that it is, on feeding it abundantly with natural soil foods, allowing the soil then to feed the plants. We have come to see that the soil is all of one piece with the life it supports. They are strong and weak together.[12]

On Walnut Acres farm, which encompasses approximately five hundred acres, the company raises an estimated 630 tons of organically grown produce annually. Since its founding, Walnut Acres has never used pesticides, herbicides, preservatives, colorings or other synthetics and observes strict crop rotation, contour farming and sheet composting. To minimize perennial pests, crops are rotated every year; the prior year's sweet-corn field is this year's oat field, next year's pea field and the following year's wheat field. The fifth year, the field is sown with alfalfa and clover seeds and lies fallow to give the earth a chance to regenerate.[13]

Keene's theory is that if we interfere with nature as little as possible, and treat her as the living thing she is, she will take care of us. He believes that it is essential to build up healthy soil to grow healthy plants, which are much less likely to be attacked by pests than weak plants. Verification of this theory came when a team of Penn State entomologists did a sweep of Walnut Acres and found no more destructive insects than a conventional farm that sprays pesticides.[14] Tim Bowser, executive director of the Pennsylvania Association for Sustainable Agriculture, points out that there is growing concern about the environmental effects of conventional agriculture. The chemical residue washed out of farmland in Central and Eastern Pennsylvania has been blamed for killing underwater grass beds in the Chesapeake Bay and, in some places, 99 percent of the oyster beds. Steve Bowes, an area organic farmer, agrees: "Farmers who use chemicals all pay for the quick fix one way or another. . . . It gets them out of the woods in the short run, but they pay the price in the long-term in the environmental impact on that farm and throughout the watershed."[15] While applying chemicals to crops may kill the insects, such a practice upsets the balance of nature, leading to an adverse reaction on desirable insects, birds and other animals.

As a natural outgrowth of its environmental sensitivity, Walnut Acres diligently looks for ways to minimize, recycle and reuse as much material as possible. It eliminated padding materials in all boxes not containing tins or glass, enabling them to use smaller boxes. The company uses two recycled paper products, "bogus" paper and newsprint, where less cushioning is required. They diplomatically pressured their bubble-wrap supplier to find recycled material such as mill scraps and post-consumer content plastic for the glass and tin packaging that needed greater protection. Walnut Acres newsletters and all forms such as invoices are printed on recycled paper. Internal recycling efforts include using paper on both sides and then donating the spent paper to the society for the blind, comprehensive composting of organic material, and extensive public education through its catalogue, parcel stuffers and direct correspondence. Packing containers of all types are reused wherever possible and paper, glass and metal materials that can not be reused are collected for recycling. The company participates in the Penn ReLeaf program, through which it sponsors the planting of three trees for every one used to print the company's catalogue. For Walnut Acres, spreading the word and helping others start the recycling effort, ". . . isn't an evangelical thing," says Bob Anderson. "It's just us."[16]

The way business at Walnut Acres grew from farming grains and vegetables to baking products and raising chickens and cattle illustrates their holistic mind set. "We raised more grain than we could really sell," explains Anderson. "So we made flour. We milled more flour than we could sell so we opened a bakery and made muffins and bread. As we made more flour there was mill waste. The logical extension of that was raising chickens and cattle who could feed on the leftovers. And from that we had manure for the fields, thus completing the circle."[17]

Other "green" policies pursued by the company include:

- Minimizing the use of electrical power through a computerized energy management system
- Staggering work hours so energy demand loads are phased in
- Encouraging employees to bring their home recyclables to the company for pickup and disposal
- Regularly inspecting all fuel tanks to ensure they are sealed and secure
- Composting all vegetable waste
- Recycling cooling water for use in irrigation
- Reusing containers whenever possible

In short, they look at virtually everything they do in the context of a complete life cycle. Under this approach management asks, "What is the long-term view of the entire process and how can we use what other people might consider to be waste or garbage in some constructive way to improve our tilling?"[18] This keeps them ahead of the curve and, therefore, there is no need for governmental regulations to prod them to do the right thing.

Respecting Those You Serve

Bob Anderson is quick to acknowledge that, just as the strength of the farm comes from their agricultural practices, the strength of their business comes from their employees and customers.[19] Thus management is very focused on the human factor. Whenever a decision needs to be made they ask themselves one simple question, "How would they want to be treated?" No new product can be sold before the family has tasted it and found it to its liking. "The basic philosophy of this company," says Anderson, "is that we'll only sell what we would put on our own tables."[20] They have a no-fault guarantee for their customers; if ever a product is found wanting it can be returned for replacement or refund, no questions asked. Anderson believes that, "The main mistake made by most companies is they pit themselves against the customer. The reality is that each of us is in a service industry. It's the quality of service that allows us to grow."[21] As most of their customers are environmentally sensitive, the company rewards them for returning the non-recyclable Styrofoam packaging required for a few products with a discount certificate worth five dollars. In short, they know their customers are key to their success and treat them accordingly.

Sharing Is Caring

Walnut Acres recognizes that every employee is a customer service representative; outstanding service is at the top of the organization's agenda. Just as they have a no-fault policy for customers, they have a no-blame policy for employees. "The only problem is the one they didn't tell us about. If there is a quality or service problem, we want to make it better immediately. We're all in this together," says Anderson.[22]

One of the criteria for employment at Walnut Acres is a willingness to work anywhere and do anything. When necessary, employees move from peeling tomatoes in the cannery to filling orders in the mail order department. Anderson believes this is a very healthy thing. People in customer service have the proper perspective of what it's like in the cannery as well as within other departments.[23] From a pragmatic standpoint, this not only keeps things moving but also eliminates the need to hire and train temporary employees during busy times.[24] The company goes to great lengths to maintain a pleasant work environment; as my wife and I toured the plant with Bob Anderson, he greeted each employee by name. Having grown up in a family of blue-collar workers, he knows that every job has dignity. With total sincerity, he expressed the feeling that the janitor's job is as important as his; for it is only by keeping the plant spotless that they can avoid the use of pesticides.

Like all companies, Walnut Acres is constantly working to improve productivity, and, not too many years ago, they installed a sophisticated computerized mail order system. In most companies, such a move would result in employee anxiety and eventual layoffs. At this company, management meets with the people who are most threatened and assures them that their expertise and loyalty are appreciated and that they all will have jobs as long as they are flexible and willing to work where needed. No one has ever been fired because of the introduction of new technology and no salaries have ever been reduced because of job switching. The efficiencies gained from the computerization were used to expand service hours and, over time, attrition has enabled the company to use their workforce more efficiently.

Walnut Acres has a generous plan for enabling its employees to participate in the financial success of the company. Through a stock appreciation plan, employees are given stock after two years of employment and additional shares are awarded annually for up to twenty years. To encourage input from all levels of the organization, three of the seven members of the Board of Directors are employees. Other more traditional benefits include flexible hours and encouraging employees to work from home when it is mutually advantageous. Anderson believes that their personnel policies have produced a motivated, loyal and productive workforce; perhaps the best proof of this is the fact that there has been virtually no employee turnover.[25]

In concluding my interview with Bob Anderson, I asked him what place spirituality played in the world of business. Without hesitation he responded:

> "I think it [spirituality] is the core of our business. . . . Part of the responsibility for taking up space or having what you have is the obligation to put back. Just as we have approached all of our agriculture so have we approached our community. The long-term approach for any business actually has to be the holistic approach or else it becomes the short-term not necessarily sustainable business."[26]

A Tough Act to Follow

It is hard to find fault with any aspect of Walnut Acres' philosophy or practices. In a number of respects, however, the company is very unusual; it has been able to distance itself from many of today's "real world" problems. Because environmental concerns received top priority since the company's founding, pollution control is a minor issue compared to what confronts most manufacturing and distribution businesses. In addition, since they are located in a relatively prosperous rural setting and draw their employees from a reasonably homogeneous population, they do not have to contend with the issue of diversity, in either its divisive or regenerative aspects. They are likewise able to avoid contentious labor-management disruptions that frequently flair up when all or part of a company's labor force is unionized. Finally, being a private company, they do not have to cater to shortsighted and often unrealistic public shareholder demands. Walnut Acres is an atypical member of the business community; both by design and circumstances their distinct characteristics have positive and negative consequences. In a positive vain, Walnut Acres has greater freedom to take progressive and somewhat controversial actions than more traditionally oriented organizations. They can, therefore, be a trendsetter for others to follow. In a negative sense, such freedom has put them so far ahead of most companies that their situation may be regarded as too utopian to be given adequate notice. To give a more rounded picture of the corporate landscape, we need to look at a company that faces many issues that Walnut Acres, largely to its credit, has been able to circumvent.

SUN COMPANY—IT'S A DIRTY BUSINESS BUT SOMEONE HAS TO DO IT

Sun Company is one of the largest independent oil refiner/gasoline marketers in the United States. The company operates five domestic refineries and markets gasoline under the Sunoco brand through approximately 3800 service stations in seventeen states. In addition, Sun sells lubricants and petrochemicals worldwide, operates pipelines and terminals domestically, and conducts coal mining and cokemaking operations in the eastern United States. Sun has revenue of over $10 billion and employs some twelve thousand people throughout the world.[27] Almost all of these businesses provide tremendous challenges with regard to environmental stewardship, and the health and safety of its employees and the surrounding community.

Sun Company officially began in 1886 when Joseph Newton Pew and Edward O. Emerson ventured into the early oil fields of Ohio. Their partnership had actually begun ten years earlier when they started a business to pipe natural gas to drilling sites in Bradford, Pennsylvania. Success with their oil leases in Ohio led to official incorporation of Sun Oil Company (Ohio) in 1890.[28] "Newton," as he was always called, was born on July 25, 1848, just eleven years before Drake drilled the world's first oil well in Titusville, Pennsylvania. The youngest of ten children born to John and Nancy Glenn Pew, he was raised on a farm in Mercer, Pennsylvania just forty miles from what was later to be the center of oil production in western Pennsylvania.[29] His family instilled in him the Presbyterian work ethic, and he was always known to his associates as a God-fearing man with an inner drive and highly developed morals.[30]

J. Howard Pew, Newton's son, had arguably the most influence on the Sun persona, as he was actively involved with the company for some seventy years. He became President in 1912 and retired as Chairman in 1970. Sun's well-known concern for the welfare of its employees was in large part a reflection of J. Howard Pew's high standards of behavior. Stories tell of him sitting by the hospital bed of an injured worker for hours because he felt personally involved. Even after forty years with the company he still knew hundreds of refinery workers personally and could ask about their children by name.[31] According to Robert Donahue, who served as Vice Chairman of Sun, "J. Howard treated his people very humanely and was really ahead of his time in many ways."[32]

Establishing Enduring Values

Because the Pews remained actively involved in the company's management for eight decades, Sun's character is imbued with their values. Those values stressed integrity, respect for others, loyalty, incentive, individual ingenuity, community and national responsibility. That spirit affected the way Sun treated its employees, conducted its negotiations, operated its daily business and interacted with people and events outside the corporation.[33] "There was never any question in my mind what they meant when they said, 'Let's do what's right.'" In fact, that phrase constantly echoed in the ear of M.D. Noble, retired President of Sun Exploration Company. In the 1930s, during the heyday of drilling East Texas oil field gushers, there were many opportunities to make quick and dirty money and many succumbed to the temptation. It was possible, for instance, to exceed the production limit set for each company by the Texas Railroad Commission. Sun could have overproduced and run hot oil but the message from Jack Pew was clear and simple: "You cheat, you're fired."

Ethical behavior was expected in all of Sun's endeavors including the sensitive antitrust area. According to Samuel K. White, the company's first general counsel, "We had very strict rules about talking with competitors about price increases. Sun was renowned in the industry for not dealing in such things. Other companies knew that." Because direction from the top has always been unequivocal in these matters, Sun has maintained a reputation for being honest, reliable and cooperative. In the rough and dirty oil industry the company has been known as one where people can make a deal on a handshake. To quote J. Colbert Peurifoy, retired manager of the company's western coal division, "We never backed out of a lease agreement even if we found out later the agreement was not in the best interests of Sun."[34] Eventually Sun's way of doing things was formalized in various statements, the two most recent being established in February 1994. One part delineated the company's purpose and the other spelled out its values. The first of these statements is re-produced below:

> Purpose: To be a source of excellence for our customers; to pro-vide a challenging professional experience for our employees; to be a rewarding investment for our shareholders; to be a re-spected citizen of community and country.

The Only Certainty . . .

Any organization that has been in operation for over one hun-dred years has seen its share of change. Sun Company has been no exception. According to Robert McClements, Jr., retired Chair-man and CEO of the company, "This company has prospered . . . sometimes by adapting to change; sometimes by embracing change; and, mostly, by initiating change."[35] While all businesses continually face changing market conditions, the fortunes of the oil industry have swung from pillar to post. In the early days, Sun enjoyed an hospitable business climate. A favorable energy market plus minimal pressure for short-term bottom line results from stockholders enabled the company to fashion policies that put people before profits. As Arch Ballou, who worked for the company for forty-six years, remembers, "For my first thirty years, it was unusual for anyone to leave." In fact, it was generally ac-cepted that if you got a job at Sun you had a job for life.[36] A spirit of partnership formed between employees and the company's management. Many progressive programs were instituted over the years, including:

- In 1926 Sun became one of the first companies in the nation to offer a stock purchase plan for employees.
- In the 1970s a management training school was founded and individual employees were made responsible for their own career advancement.
- Sun was the first company in the oil industry to open up the job-bidding system and to introduce outplacement counseling.

- In 1996, recognizing the increasing need and desire of its employees for part-time work, Sun established a policy that would enable eligible employees to continue receiving full medical and dental coverage paid for entirely by the company.

As expressed by Bill Rutherford, former human resources senior vice president, "Helping people use their talent more fully and make their own decisions carries on the Sun tradition of caring about people."[37]

After the spike in oil and gas prices in the mid to late 1970s, the energy industry experienced some difficult times. By the early 1980s it became obvious that a more flexible management style and solidified financial structure were required if Sun was to remain an industry leader. Energy companies began to reduce employment levels and change organizational structures. Sun was no different; its style needed to keep evolving with the times. As Robert H. Campbell, currently Chairman of the Board, stated more than ten years ago:

> Any company that doesn't recognize the competitiveness of today's world will not be around for a one hundredth anniversary. But I'll still contend that even through all the changes, Sun has maintained its traditional values.[38]

Self-Discovery—Level II

As we have seen in prior chapters, companies are living organizations composed of living organisms (their employees). Therefore, it is just as important for corporations that want to maximize their potential to engage in introspective activities as it is for individuals. The importance of this exercise was acknowledged in the Sun publication, *Centennial Celebration: The Story of Sun Company*, which was published in 1986 to commemorate the company's one hundredth anniversary. As quoted in that publication:

> To enjoy a future as privileged as the past, Sun will have to at-
> tend carefully to the present and look confidently to the future.
> For that task Sun will do well to *know itself*.[39] (emphasis added)

To remain financially strong and competitively viable, companies need to reinvent themselves continually. This may neces-
sitate acquisitions, divestitures and/or structural reorganizations.
In 1988 Sun made a significant strategic change when it distributed total ownership in its United States oil and gas exploration
and production subsidiary to its shareholders. The next several
years witnessed a precipitous decline in earnings. In fact, the
company's average return on capital for much of the 1990s has
been below what could have been earned on virtually risk-free
United States Treasury Bonds.

A major overhaul was needed. Changing times necessitated
that the company scrutinize itself inside and out. This included
its financial structure, its customers' needs, the optimal size and
productivity of both its union and nonunion labor force, and the
strength and characteristics of its competitors. In mid-1995, after
months of analysis, significant adjustments were made. About
eight hundred salaried employees, representing close to 30 percent of the targeted work force, were laid off. Affected employees included accountants, public relations officials, computer
technicians, payroll clerks and administrative personnel. Some of
the work was eliminated and some was assigned to outside contractors. In addition, the company cut its debt level and dividend
payout.[40]

In an unprecedented and psychologically difficult agreement, the Philadelphia Area Building Trades Union, which supports Sun's contract work, agreed to a three-year deal that
reduced members' pay by 10 percent and created more flexible
working conditions. In return, Sun committed to hire only unionized contractors. This highly unusual "give-back" on the part of
the union was made possible when the union was shown credi-
ble information that their members wages were as much as 35
percent higher than labor rates paid by competitors. Patrick Gilles-

pie, the business manager of the council that represents the unions said "the unions agreed to the concessions in the spirit of cooperation intended to make Sun Co. more competitive in today's environment." He went on to say that since 1982, when Sun hired a nonunion contractor at one of its refineries, there had been much animosity between the two parties. After many years and much introspection the two former adversaries studied each other's needs and came to an agreement that can meet the requirements of both sides.[41]

One of the keys to self-knowledge, whether on the individual or the organizational level, is to study one's needs and desires in a detached and objective manner, and then prioritize them. With the vast majority of Sun's revenues coming from refining and marketing, satisfying the end user, the driving public, must be high on the priority list. To indicate its importance, Sun introduced its "CustomerFirst" initiative in 1994. The major components of this effort are: a Customer Satisfaction Index to measure how customers feel about buying at Sunoco; a Business Process Mapping model to ensure that all decisions connected with the Sunoco brand are made with the customer in mind; and a toll-free customer response number.[42] In 1995 the company introduced the Customer BEST (Building Exceptional Service Together) program in conjunction with its service station dealers. Sun recognizes that providing superior service is critical to meeting their long-term strategic goals and they certainly appear to be giving their customers a high level of attention. Segments of Sun's business that have a more tenuous bottom line connection have traditionally received less time and fewer resources. What have been the consequences?

Sowing and Reaping

Sun's operations, particularly coal mining and oil exploration, refining and marketing, expose the company to potentially serious health, environmental and safety (HES) problems. It is fair to say that, until fairly recently, pollution control and environmental stewardship have not been a top priority for the large integrated energy companies. In Sun's case, it was not until around 1960, seventy-four years after the company's founding, that formal policies regarding any HES function were formally established. Thus the company has had to play catch up over the past several decades to reverse a number of festering problems. Sun first established a policy dealing with the environment in 1982. In 1990 two additional policies were adopted entitled, *Sun, "What We Believe" Safety, Health and the Environment* and *Sun Health, Environmental and Safety Policy*. It was 1993, however, before their policies turned from predominately defensive to clearly proactive. In February 1993, Sun became the first company in the Fortune 500 to endorse the CERES principles. It takes true leadership and vision to place a company in a position where it can be easily judged. In the words of Robert Campbell:

> . . . in February 1993, we embarked on a long journey to change the way we behave in matters of environmental protection and workplace health and safety. It's not that these weren't important priorities in years past. It's just that the world we operate in is changing, and we need to change our behavior to meet increasing external expectations. . . . Sun people were exposed to non-traditional stakeholders and their viewpoints. The exposure not only caused us to "push the envelope" but also provided opportunities to influence others.[43]

In making a commitment to improve its environmental performance and be publicly accountable for that improvement, Sun took on a significant public relations risk. In 1994 there were more than 240 Health, Environmental and Safety personnel with approximately seventy-five involved in specific environmental areas such as waste management, pollution prevention, waste minimization, air quality, permitting and remediation management. While HES might have been an inviting target for Sun's 1995 downsizing, the department actually absorbed slightly less of a reduction in employment than many other parts of the organization.

Accountability is a critical part of improving HES performance. To help ensure compliance, Sun's business unit leaders must make quarterly HES performance reports and review serious incidents with the executive-level HES Committee. Moreover, senior managers meet regularly with their senior vice presidents to discuss significant HES issues. HES performance has become a growing part of salary reviews as well as bonus recommendations and promotions. To help assure continuous improvement, Sun developed extensive performance standards which will enable them to delineate future benchmarks for all of their core businesses. Stated objectives range from tracking annual goals to establishing specific performance measurements. By establishing definite standards, Sun has formalized its commitment not only to CERES, but to the Chemical Manufacturers Association's Responsible Care, the National Petroleum Refiner's Association's BEST and the American Petroleum Institute's STEP programs as well.[44]

Sun's Health, Environment and Safety Review is combined with its annual CERES Report. It is approximately forty pages in length and discusses the following relevant topics:

- Environmental Policies, Organization and Management
- Materials Policy
- Releases to the Environment
- Waste Management
- Use of Energy
- Workplace Health and Safety
- Emergency Response and Public Disclosure
- Product Stewardship
- Supplier Relationships
- Health, Safety and Environmental Audits
- Compliance

To measure its performance, Sun compares its targeted objectives against actual results in key areas such as oil spills, toxic emissions, permit exceedences of air emissions and wastewater discharge, Occupational Safety and Health Administration (OSHA) recordable incident rate, energy conservation, incident prevention and fire loss. Accomplishments and challenges are forthrightly noted. For instance, Sun reduced its toxic emissions for eight consecutive years. Sun and the Pennsylvania Department of Environmental Resources initiated a collaborative study to identify ways to accomplish environmental compliance in a more cost-effective manner. A laser printer toner program that recycles and reuses old toner cartridges was initiated. Reimbursements for the returned cartridges are donated to Earthright, a non-profit organization promoting conservation and non-polluting waste management.

Despite many accomplishments, much work is still to be done. J. Robert Banks, the Vice President in charge of HES, noted in an interview a number of broad areas where the company faces challenges. Areas needing further effort include the company's community relations activities, its desire to get employees at all levels committed to HES performance improvements, the quantifying of financial benefits that have been derived from HES practices, and establishing formalized life cycle analysis for all their products so that all costs are accounted for beginning at the products conception and ending with its ultimate disposal.[45]

Endorsing the CERES Principles has resulted in a number of tangible benefits for Sun, according to Bob Banks. The company has had exposure to a variety of previously unrepresented views which has helped them in designing their performance standards and has led to a better understanding of community concerns and objectives. When a local environmental group threatened legal action because of an incident at one of their facilities, the company met with the group and was able to defuse the situation by convincing them that Sun was committed to avoiding such problems in the future. Because they were the first Fortune 500 company to endorse the CERES Principles, Sun has assumed a leadership position in this arena and is now in a position to influence the relationship between environmentalists and businesses. Socially responsible investors, whether individual or institutional participants, are now likely to include Sun on their list of acceptable investments as long as the company's financial performance also meets their targets.

CERES has a vested interest in seeing Sun succeed and Sun would like to see CERES endorsed by a growing number of businesses. It's a win/win partnership that should accrue to the benefit of both parties. While there will be ups and downs in this as in all relationships, Sun has demonstrated its desire to achieve continuous improvement and has made itself publicly accountable by reporting its performance, both the pretty and the ugly, in an annual audit. By taking the initiative, Sun is setting an example that deserves emulation. Unless businesses worldwide make environmental concerns a high priority, our day of reckoning will grow uncomfortably close. Such a commitment need not be thought of as an onerous or debilitating chore. According to Campbell: "We have never had a moment of regret about it [endorsing CERES]. Every piece of mail, every telephone call, every in person contact I've had from shareholders has praised the decision to go ahead with the agreement." In addition, Sun's adherence to the Principles evoked a feeling of pride from the company's employees "and a renewed sense of determination to improve our performance."[46]

THE EARTH, THE SUN AND HERMES

Walnut Acres and Sun Company have more things in common than might be readily apparent. Both of the company's founders were in the forefront of the creation of new industries. Visionaries Paul Keene and Joseph Pew displayed considerable courage, dedication and perseverance to make their dreams a reality. In addition, both companies are in businesses closely tied to the earth's natural resources. Of more immediate relevance, the history of these two companies is replete with outstanding examples of the seven Hermetic Principles at work.

Both Walnut Acres and Sun were founded by individuals with a steadfast set of values. Unwavering reverence for the sanctity of the earth and strict adherence to high moral and ethical standards are both essentially cerebral concepts that exemplify The Principal of Mentalism. All acts of creation are based on archetypal ideals that are fundamentally mental in character.

The Principle of Vibration tells us that everything vibrates, everything moves, nothing rests. This universal condition of ceaseless change is evident throughout the history of both companies. In the case of Sun, the changing fortunes of the oil industry are a salient example. From frugal beginnings, it was not too many years before the company reached a high level of profitability. Their situation has now come full circle. Losses or low levels of profitability through most of the 1990s finally gave way to a very profitable 1997. Walnut Acres, which had a near monopoly position in the Mid-Atlantic region of the United States for many years, is now facing considerable competition. Demand for organically grown food has mushroomed and drawn new competitors into the field. This good news/bad news situation means that the company must now begin the costly process of developing new channels of distribution to keep old customers and reach a potentially larger base of new ones. When we accept change as an inevitable and natural part of life, we begin to "go with the flow" rather than trying to do the impossible and maintain the status quo. By adopting a more flexible mind set we actually enhance our receptivity to the riches the universe so magnanimously dispenses.

To be truly successful we must be introspective; "know thyself." Because everything in the universe is mental and originates as a thought, the mental acuity attained in the pursuit of self-knowledge enhances our ability to understand and relate to all other parts of the universe. Because Paul Keene knew that the life force in the soil was the same energy as that found in humanity itself, he treated the earth with the same reverence he extended to all other living things. Understanding The Principle of Correspondence has paid handsome dividends for the company. Sun, by undergoing periodic self-examinations, has become increasingly aware of and attuned to the needs of its various constituencies; its investors, customers, employees, and suppliers, as well as the community and the environment. "Know One, Know All," is an important teaching of arcane philosophy.

The Principles of Rhythm and Polarity are closely related. Walnut Acres had to learn to pay close attention to and make preparations for the rhythm of the seasons as well as the daily vagaries of the weather. Sun is also affected by these two principles in a variety of ways. One obvious example is the company's relationship with its unions. There have been conspicuous fluctuations in their relationship, as the parties vacillate between confrontation and cooperation.

The Principle of Cause and Effect is clearly evident when the environmental policies of the two companies are examined. Walnut Acres has always followed the philosophy of giving back to the earth more than it has taken away. Although not immune from weather problems, Walnut Acres has reaped the rewards of the earth's generosity. Conversely, Sun did not always place the environment at the top of its priority list and may now have to devote a larger proportion of its resources to environmental projects than would otherwise have been necessary. ". . . for whatever a man sows, that he will also reap."[47]

The Principle of Gender states that everything has both masculine and feminine characteristics. The former include active, projective, analytic and separating attributes while the latter encompass passive, receptive, synthetic and unifying qualities. Both companies, although somewhat paternalistic from the beginning, have shown a reasonable balance between the two principles. Sun's history of caring for and sharing with its employees has helped foster a family atmosphere. Walnut Acres' respect for and nurturing of Gaia has been repaid with bountiful harvests as well as loyal employees and trusting customers. With the competitive climate intense for both companies, Walnut Acres may have to accentuate the dynamic masculine element as it attempts to expand its business. On the other hand, Sun must remain vigilant that its restructuring exigencies do not obscure the universal need for the feminine attribute of compassion.

Business, with its global influence and its ability to adapt rapidly to changing conditions, has become one of the most effective vehicles for accelerating our self-conscious awareness. In an effort to retain highly trained work forces and show customers they are responsible corporate citizens, business organizations are increasingly receptive to the changing desires of their various constituencies. As new technology brings the countries of the world closer together, the interconnectedness of all things is inescapable. The benefits of holistic thinking are gaining recognition as the superficial appearance of separation is being replaced by a realization that each of us is inextricably united with all of life. Everyone's well being is dependent on the health and vitality of all other parts. An intent of this book has been to illustrate how employees, the soul of all businesses, have been moving into alignment with universal laws and principles. The critical mass required to reverse humanity's separatist thinking and to transform behavior so that it is in full accord with the underlying unity is closer than generally believed. When sufficiently established, a more compassionate and enlightened society will unfold. The world of commerce is playing a vital role in humanity's transition to higher levels of consciousness.

His work of sowing seeds completed, Hermes left this note on the boardroom table to remind us of his seven principles:

LIFE IS THOUGHT . . . CONTEMPLATE IT
LIFE IS VARIETY . . . REVEL IN IT
LIFE IS SYNCRONISTIC . . . PRAISE IT
LIFE IS CREATIVE . . . UNFOLD IT
LIFE IS DUALISTIC . . . BALANCE IT
LIFE IS FLOW . . . ADAPT TO IT
LIFE IS GENERATIVE . . . RENEW IT

These principles are the key to *REAL PROSPERITY*.

NOTES

1. Joan Bavaria. "CERES at Five: Just Beginning!" *CERES ON PRINCIPLE*, 3 (Summer 1994): p. 1.

2. Kerry Hannon. "Pure and Unadulterated," *U.S. News & World Report*, 15 May 1995, p. 86.

3. Walnut Acres Organic Farms, *Holiday Celebration 1995*, Penns Creek, PA, p. 2.

4. Paul Keene. "The Grandfather of Organic Gardening," interview by Joanne Leigh Brand, *Lightworks*, August 1993, p. 25.

5. Beverly Groff. "Farmer's Essays Sown Together," review of *Fear Not to Sow*, by Paul Keene, ed., Dorothy Seymour, *Reading (PA) Eagle*, 19 February 1989, p. 14(E).

6. Keene. "The Grandfather of Organic Gardening," p. 25.

7. Groff, p. 14(E).

8. Carole Sugarman. "Keeping the Faith at Walnut Acres," *Washington Post*, 7 August 1991, p. 4(E).

9. Keene. "The Grandfather of Organic Gardening," p. 26.

10. Steve Kennedy. "Real Farm," *Apprise*, May 1995, p. 41.

11. Joanna Poncavage. "The Farm That Gandhi Grew," *Organic Gardening*, February 1991, p. 58.

12. Groff, p. 14(E).

13. Hannon, p. 91.

14. "Organic Expert Shares Advice," *Harrisburg Patriot*, 10 August 1995, p. 7(C).

15. Don Hopey. "Singing Harmony with Nature," *Pittsburgh Post-Gazette*, 23 August 1993, p. 10(A).

16. Virginia Simon. "A Commitment to the Earth," *Target Marketing*, January 1993, p. 25.

17. Joe Butkiewicz. "The Good Earth," *Wilkes-Barre (PA) Times-Leader*, 23 June 1991, p. 1(G).

18. Robert Anderson, President, Walnut Acres, interview by author, 18 October 1995, Penns Creek, Pennsylvania, tape recording.

19. Gail Strock. "Walnut Acres a Major Player in Organic Foods Industry," *Pennsylvania Business Central*, 26 May–8 June 1995, p. 16.

20. Ibid.

21. Ibid.

22. Ibid.

23. Kennedy, p. 41.

24. Leah Ingram. "Down on the Farm," *Entrepreneur*, April 1994, p. 168.

25. Robert Anderson, interview by author.

26. Ibid.

27. Sun Company, Inc., *1996 Annual Report* (Philadelphia), pp. 3–4.

28. *Centennial Celebration: The Story of Sun Company* (Philadelphia: Sun Company, Inc.), pp. 10–11.

29. Ibid, p. 13.

30. Ibid, p. 8.

31. Ibid, p. 20.

32. Ibid, p. 84.

33. Ibid, p. 77.

34. Ibid, pp. 88–89.

35. Ibid, p. 25.

36. Ibid, p. 83.

37. Ibid, p. 75.

38. Ibid, p. 84.

39. Ibid, p. 78.

40. Andrew Maykuth. "Sun Will Cut its Staff and its Dividend," *Philadelphia Inquirer*, 14 June 1995, p. 1(C).

41. Andrew Maykuth. "Unions Agree to Take Cut in Pay at Sun," *Philadelphia Inquirer*, 26 October 1995, p. 1(C).

42. Sun 1994 Annual Report, p. 9.

43. Sun Company, Inc., *Health, Environment and Safety: 1993 Progress Report*, p. 1.

44. Sun Company, Inc., *Health, Environment and Safety Review and CERES Report: 1994*, p. 5.

45. J. Robert Banks, Vice President, HES, Sun Company, Inc., interview by author, 12 April 1996, Philadelphia, Pennsylvania.

46. Whitman Bassow, Ph.D., "CERES Principles are Worth Exploring," *Environmental Protection*, June 1994, p. 10.

47. Galatians 6:7 (Revised Standard Version).

Bibliography

Achstatter, Gerard A. "Prescription for Success: Change Fast—and Often." *Investor's Business Daily*, 2 May 1996.

"Apocalypse—But Not Just Now," *Financial Times*, 4 January 1993.

Ashbery, John. "A Last Word from a Poet," *Forbes*, 14 September 1992.

Augros, Robert and George Stanciu. "The New Biology," *Noetic Sciences Review*, Winter 1989.

Baird, Kristen. "Modern Family Concerns Show up in Company Policies," *Small Business News (Philadelphia)*, December 1994.

Baskin, Ken. "Is Your Business Alive?" *Business Philadelphia*, November 1994.

Bassow, Whitman. "CERES Principles are Worth Exploring," *Environmental Protection*, June 1994.

Bavaria, Joan. "CERES at Five: Just Beginning!" *CERES ON PRINCIPLE* 3 (Summer 1994).

Bennett, Michael E. "The Saturn Corporation: New Management-Union Partnership at the Factory of the Future." *Looking Ahead*, XIII, 4 (April 1992). Reproduced by Saturn Corporation, Spring Hill, TN.

Bezi, Robert and George H. Gallup, Jr. "Seeking Spiritual Renewal," *Philadelphia Inquirer*, 25 December 1994.

Blanchard, Kenneth H. "Ethics in American Business." In *New Traditions in Business: Spirit and Leadership in the 21st Century*, ed. John Renesch. San Francisco: Berrett-Koehler Publishers, 1992.

Bleakley, Fred R. "Strange Bedfellows," *Wall Street Journal*, 13 January 1995.

Bohm, David. *Wholeness and the Implicate Order*. London: Routledge Kegan Paul Ltd., 1980.

Bohm, D. and B. Hiley. "On the Intuitive Understanding of Nonlocality as Implied by Quantum Theory," *Foundations of Physics* 5 (1975).

Brennan, Barbara. *Light Emerging*. New York: Bantam Books, 1993.

Breton, Denise and Christopher Largent. *The Soul of Economies: Spiritual Evolution Goes to the Marketplace*. Wilmington, DE: Idea House Publishing Co., 1991.

Bronowski, Jacob. "Black Magic and White Magic." In *The World Treasury of Physics, Astronomy and Mathematics*. Edited by Timothy Ferris. With a Foreword by Clifton Fadiman, genl. ed. Boston: Little, Brown & Co., 1991.

Brown, Rosemary, ed. *Co-op America's National Green Pages*. Washington: Co-op America, 1996.

Buber, Martin, ed. *Tales of the Hasidim*. rev. ed. in 1 vol. New York: Shocken Books, 1975.

Bunker, Dusty. *Quintiles and Trediciles: The Geometry of the Goddess*. West Chester, PA: Whitford Press, a division of Schiffer Publishing Ltd., 1989.

Business for Social Responsibility Fact Sheet. San Francisco: Business for Social Responsibility, March 1995.

Butkiewicz, Joe. "The Good Earth." *Wilkes-Barre (PA) Times-Leader*, 23 June 1991.

Byrom, T. *The Dhammapada: The Sayings of the Buddha*. Quoted in Roger N. Walsh and Frances Vaughan, eds., *Beyond Ego: Transpersonal Dimensions in Psychology*. Los Angeles: Jeremy P. Tarcher, 1980.

Campbell, Joseph, ed. *The Portable Jung*. New York: Penguin Books, 1976.

" 'Can One Sell the Sky?' Indian Asks," *Salt Lake Tribune*, 6 June 1976.

Capra, Fritjof. *The Tao of Physics*. New York: Bantam Books, 1975.

Case, Paul Foster. *The Book of Tokens*. Los Angeles: Builders of the Adytum, 1989.

_____. *The Tarot, A Key to the Wisdom of the Ages*. Richmond: Macoy Publishing Co., 1947.

_____. *The True and Invisible Rosicrucian Order*. York Beach, ME: Samuel Weiser, Inc., 1975.

"CEO Sees Business as the Engine for Social Transformation." *The New Leaders*, January/February 1995.

Claire, Thomas. *Bodywork: What Type of Massage to Get—and How to Make the Most of It*. New York: William Morrow & Co., 1995.

Cleaver, Joanne. "The Spirit of Success." *Home Office Computing*, May 1996.

Cohen, J. M. and J-F. Phipps, ed. *The Common Experience*. Los Angeles: Jeremy P. Tarcher, 1979.

Cole, K. C. *Sympathetic Vibrations: Reflections on Physics as a Way of Life*. With a Foreword by Frank Oppenheimer. New York: Bantam Books, 1985.

Compass:The Newsletter of The Natural Step 2 (Fall 1996).

Davies, Paul. *God and the New Physics*. New York: Simon & Schuster, 1983.

Dobrzynski, Judith H. "An Inside Look at CalPERS Boardroom Report Card," *Business Week*, 17 October 1994.

Dossey, Larry, M.D. *Healing Words: The Power of Prayer and the Practice of Medicine*. San Francisco: HarperSanFrancisco, 1993.

Ehrlich, Paul. *The Population Bomb*. New York: Ballantine Books, 1968.

Eisenstein, Paul A. "GM Saturn's Hudler: On Treating People Right from Shop Floor to Showroom," *Investor's Business Daily*, 20 December 1996.

Emery, Marcia. "Intuition: The Spark that Ignites Vision," *The New Leaders*, January/February 1995.

Faivre, Antoine. *The Eternal Hermes: From Greek God to Alchemical Magus*. Translated by Joscelyn Godwin. Grand Rapids, MI: Phanes Press, 1995.

Fenske, Elizabeth W., ed. *Spiritual Insights for Daily Living*. Independence, MO: Independence Press for Spiritual Frontiers Fellowship, 1986.

Fierman, Jaclyn. "Winning Ideas from Maverick Managers," *Fortune*, 6 February 1995.

Filipczak, Bob. "25 Years of Diversity at UPS," *Training Magazine*, August 1992.

"French Executive Scouts for New Business Ideas," *The New Leaders*, November/December 1995.

Frenier, Carol R. *Business and The Feminine Principle: The Untapped Resource*. Boston: Butterworth–Heinemann, 1997.

Fried, John J. "Firms Take into Account Pollution Practices," *Philadelphia Inquirer*, 20 February 1995.

_____. "Saving the Earth, and They Mean Business," *Philadelphia Inquirer*, 18 December 1994.

Friedman, Dana E. and Ellen Galinsky. *Work and Family Trends.* New York: Families and Work Institute, 1991.

Fuhrman, Peter and Michael Schuman. "Now We Are Our Own Masters," *Forbes*, 23 May 1994.

Galen, Michele and Karen West. "Companies Hit the Road Less Traveled," *Business Week*, 5 June 1995.

Galen, Michele with Ann Therese Palmer. "Diversity: Beyond the Numbers Game," *Business Week*, 24 August 1995.

Galinsky, Ellen and Peter J. Stein. "The Impact of Human Resource Policies on Employees: Balancing Work/Family Life," *Journal of Family Issues* 11 (December 1990).

Gaouette, Nicole. "Do-Good Investing Is Doing Good," *Philadelphia Inquirer*, 7 June 1996.

Glassman, James K. " 'Ethical' Stocks Don't Have To Be Downers," *Washington Post*, 23 April 1995.

Goleman, Daniel. "Holographic Memory: Karl Pribram Interviewed by Daniel Goleman," *Psychology Today*, February 1979.

"Good Citizens," *Investor's Business Daily*, 17 May 1996.

Gottlieb, Dan. "On Healing," *Philadelphia Inquirer*, 19 June 1995.

Great Religions of the World. New York: National Geographic Book Service, 1978.

Greenwald, John. "Magellan's New Direction." *Time*, 3 June 1996.

Groff, Beverly. "Farmer's Essays Sown Together," Review of *Fear Not to Sow* by Paul Keene, ed. Dorothy Seymour. *Reading (PA) Eagle*, 19 February 1989.

Groves, Martha and Stuart Silverstein."Levi Strauss Tailors a Deal to Suit its Workers." *Philadelphia Inquirer*, 7 June 1996.

Guiley, Rosemary Ellen. *The Encyclopedia of Dreams: Symbols and Interpretations.* New York: Berkley Books, 1995.

Hall, Manly P. *The Secret Teachings of All Ages: An Encyclopedic Outline of Masonic, Hermetic, Qabbalistic and Rosicrucian Symbolical Philosophy.* Golden Anniversary Edition. The Philosophical Research Society, Inc., 1977.

Hamilton, J. G. DeRoulhac, ed. *The Best Letters of Thomas Jefferson.* Cambridge: Riverside Press, 1926.

Hannon, Kerry. "Pure and Unadulterated," *U.S. News & World Report*, 15 May 1995.

Harman, Willis W. *Global Mind Change: The Promise of the Last Years of the Twentieth Century.* Indianapolis: Knowledge Systems Inc. for the Institute of Noetic Sciences, 1988.

Harms, Valerie. *The National Audubon Society Almanac of the Environment: The Ecology of Everyday Life.* New York: G.P. Putnam's Sons, 1994.

Havel, Vaclav. Speech on the Occasion of the Liberty Medal Ceremony. Philadelphia, 4 July 1994.

Hay, Louise L. *You Can Heal Your Life.* Santa Monica CA: Hay House, 1984.

Honan, William H. "Of Spielberg, Berra and (Many) Other Graduation Greats," *New York Times,* 17 May 1996.

Hopey, Don. "Singing Harmony with Nature," *Pittsburgh Post-Gazette,* 23 August 1993.

"How Nonprofits Help Companies Mind Their Waste," *BSR Update: A Publication of Business for Social Responsibility,* June 1996.

Huxley, Aldous. *The Perennial Philosophy.* New York: Harper & Row, 1945.

Important Dates in Saturn History. Spring Hill, TN: Saturn Corporation, 1995.

Ingram, Leah. "Down on the Farm." *Entrepreneur,* April 1994.

Integrity Agreement: LawForms Uniform Agreement Establishing Procedures for Settling Disputes. G-4a. LawForms 4-80, 3-87.

Jackson, Phil and Hugh Delehanty. *Sacred Hoops: Spiritual Lessons of a Hardwood Warrior.* With a Foreword by Senator Bill Bradley. New York: Hyperion, 1995.

"J.D. Power Initial Quality Rankings," *USA Today,* 8 May 1996.

Joba, Cynthia, Herman Bryant Maynard Jr. and Michael Ray. "Competition, Cooperation and Co-Creation: Insights From the World Business Academy." In *The New Paradigm in Business: Emerging Strategies for Leadership and Organizational Change.* Edited by Michael Ray and Alan Rinzler. New York: Putnam Publishing Group for the World Business Academy, 1993.

Johnson, Edward C., II. "Contrary Opinion in Stock Market Techniques." In *Classics: An Investor's Anthology.* Edited by Charles D. Ellis with James R. Vertin. Homewood IL: Business One Irwin, 1989.

Jones, Del. "Companies Have to Do a Balancing Act," *USA TODAY,* 15 May 1995.

_____. "Companies Won't Derail Diversity," *USA TODAY*, 15 May 1995.

Kantrowitz, Barbara. "Search for the Sacred," *Newsweek*, 28 November 1994.

Kaplan, Aryeh. *Meditation and Kabbalah*. York Beach, ME: Samuel Weiser, 1982.

Keene, Paul. "The Grandfather of Organic Gardening." Interview by Joanne Leigh Brand. *Lightworks*, August 1993.

Kelly, Marjorie. "The President as Poet: An Intimate Conversation with Jim Autry," In *The New Paradigm in Business: Emerging Strategies for Leadership and Organizational Change*. Edited by Michael Ray and Alan Rinzler. New York: Putnam Publishing Group for the World Business Academy, 1993.

Kennedy, Steve. "Real Farm," *Apprise*, May 1995.

Keyes, Ken. *Handbook to Higher Consciousness*. Berkeley, CA: Living Love Center, 1973.

Kinder, Peter, Steven D. Lydenberg, and Amy L. Domini. *Investing for Good: Making Money While Being Socially Responsible*. New York: HarperCollins, 1993.

Kline, Morris. *Mathematics and the Search for Knowledge*. New York: Oxford University Press, 1985.

Kohn, Alfie. "The Case Against Competition," *Noetic Sciences Collection 1980 to 1990*.

Koretz, Gene. "How Many Hours in a Workweek?" *Business Week*, 16 June 1997.

_____. "Yankees: Nose to the Grindstone," *Business Week*, 4 September 1995.

Koselka, Rita. "Babies Are Welcome," *Forbes*, 24 April 1995.

Kripalani, Krishna. *All Men Are Brothers: Autobiographical Reflections*. New York: Continuum, 1994.

Landers, Jim. " 'Gasoline to Hit $4 per Gallon,' Specialist Says," *Dallas Morning News*, 2 May 1981.

Leanna, Carrie R. "Why Downsizing Is Bad for Business." *Philadelphia Inquirer*, 5 January 1996.

Lee, William H. *Coenzyme Q-10: Is It Our New Fountain of Youth? A Good Health Guide*. Edited by Richard A. Passwater and Earl Mindell. New Canaan, CT: Keats Publishing, 1987.

LeFauve, Richard G. "The Saturn Corporation: A Balance of People, Technology and Business Systems." *Looking Ahead*, XIII, 4 (April 1992). Reproduced by Saturn Corporation, Spring Hill, TN.

LeShan, Lawrence. *How to Meditate*. New York: Bantam Books, 1974.

Linden, Dana Wechsler and Bruce Upbin. "Boy Scouts on a Rampage." *Forbes*, 1 January 1996.

Liungman, Carl G. *Dictionary of Symbols*. Santa Barbara, CA: ABC-CLIO, 1991.

Lynch, Timothy. *Polluting Our Principles: Environmental Prosecutions and the Bill of Rights*. Policy Analysis 223. Washington: The Cato Institute, 1995.

Malkiel, Burton G. "Socially Responsible Investing," In *Classics II: Another Investor's Anthology*. Edited by Charles D. Ellis with James R. Vertin. Homewood IL: Business One Irwin, 1991.

Malthus, Thomas Robert. *On Population*. Edited by Gertrude Himmelfarb. The Modern Library. New York: Random House, 1960.

Markowitz, Elliot. "Dwyer Claims JWP Down but Not Out," *Computer Reseller News*, 26 October 1992.

"Marriot Program Helps Low-Wage Workers Cope," *BSR Update: A Publication of Business for Social Responsibility*, August–September 1996.

Maykuth, Andrew, "Sun Will Cut Its Staff and Its Dividend," *Philadelphia Inquirer*, 14 June 1995.

_____. "Unions Agree to Take Cut in Pay at Sun," *Philadelphia Inquirer*, 26 October 1995.

Merline, John. "Corporations at the Trough?" *Investor's Business Daily*, 12 March 1996.

Milanovich, Norma and Shirley McCune. *The Light Shall Set You Free*. Albuquerque, NM: Athena Publishing, 1996.

Milbank, Dana, Valerie Reitman, Dianne Solis, and Paulette Thomas. "Women in Business: A Global Report Card," *Wall Street Journal*, 26 July 1995.

Millman, Dan. *The Warrior Athlete: Body, Mind and Spirit*. Walpole, NH: Stillpoint Publishing, 1979.

Minard, Lawrence. "The Principle of Maximum Pessimism," *Forbes*, 16 January 1995.

Mitchell, Russell and Michael Oneal. "Managing by Values: Is Levi Strauss' Approach Visionary—or Flaky?" *Business Week*, 1 August 1994.

Moore, Daphna. *The Rabbi's Tarot: Spiritual Secrets of the Tarot.* St. Paul: Llewellyn Publications, a division of Llewellyn Worldwide, Ltd., 1989.

Moore, Stephen and Dean Stansel. *How Corporate Welfare Won.* Policy Analysis 254. Washington: The Cato Institute, 1996.

Morgan, Marlo. *Mutant Message Downunder.* Lees Summit, MO: MM Co., 1991.

Naisbitt, John. *Global Paradox.* New York: Avon Books, 1994.

Needleman, Jacob. *Money and the Meaning of Life.* New York: Doubleday, a division of Bantam Doubleday Dell Publishing Group, 1991.

Nomani, Asra Q. "CalPERS Says Its Investment Decisions Will Reflect How Firms Treat Workers," *Wall Street Journal,* 16 June 1994.

Norris, Floyd. "Market Place," *New York Times,* 22 September 1995.

Novak, Philip. *The World's Wisdom: Sacred Texts of the World's Religions.* San Francisco: HarperCollins, 1994.

The One and the Many. Chicago: A. C. McClurg & Co., 1909.

Oppenheimer, Robert J. *Science and the Common Understanding.* New York: Oxford University Press, 1954.

"Organic Expert Shares Advice," *Harrisburg Patriot,* 10 August 1995.

O'Toole, Jack and Jim Lewandowski. "Forming the Future: The Marriage of People and Technology at Saturn." Presented to Stanford University Industrial Engineering and Engineering Management. Palo Alto, CA, 29 March 1990. Reproduced by Saturn Corporation, Spring Hill, TN.

Pennar, Karen. "Why Investors Stampede," *Business Week,* 13 February 1995.

Pereira, Joseph. "The Healing Power of Prayer Is Tested by Science," *Wall Street Journal,* 20 December 1995.

Pierrakos, Eva. *The Pathwork of Self-Transformation.* Compiled and edited by Judith Saly. New York: Bantam Books, 1990.

Plato. *The Dialogues,* Vol. IV, Laws X. Translated by B. Jowett. 4th ed. Oxford: Clarendon Press, 1964.

Poncavage, Joanna. "The Farm That Gandhi Grew," *Organic Gardening,* February 1991.

Postrel, Virginia I. "It's All in the Head," *Forbes ASAP,* 26 February 1996.

Prabhavananda, Swami and Christopher Isherwood, trans. *How to Know God: The Yogi Aphorisms of Patanjali*. New York: Mentor Books, 1969.

Rama, Swami. *Perennial Psychology of the Bhagavad Gita*. Honesdale, PA: Himalayan International Institute, 1985.

Rapoport, Rhona and Lotte Bailyn. *Relinking Life and Work: Toward a Better Future*. New York: The Ford Foundation, 1996.

Rifkin, Jeremy. *The End of Work: The Decline of the Global Labor Force and the Dawn of the Post-Market Era*. New York: Jeremy P. Tarcher/Putnam Books, 1995.

Roddick, Anita. "Anita Roddick Speaks Out on Corporate Responsibility," *The Body Shop Lectures II*. West Sussex: The Body Shop International plc, 1994.

Rosen, Robert H. "The Anatomy of a Healthy Company." In *New Traditions in Business: Spirit and Leadership in the 21st Century*, ed. John Renesch. San Francisco: Berrett-Koehler Publishers, 1992.

Rouse, Ewart. "Book Chains Escalate War of Supremacy," *Philadelphia Inquirer*, 22 April 1996.

Rubin, Paul H. "The High Cost of Lawsuits," *Investor's Business Daily*, 4 March 1996.

Rudnick, David. "Cents & Sensibility," *Business Life: The Magazine for Europe*, February 1997.

Russell, Peter. "A Shift in Consciousness: Implications for Business." Interview by Willis Harman. *World Business Academy Perspectives* 9, no 4 (1995).

Rutledge, John. "The Portrait on My Office Wall," *Forbes*, 30 December 1996.

Rybczynski, Witold. *Waiting for the Weekend*. New York: Viking Penguin, 1991.

Samuelson, Paul A. *Economics: An Introductory Analysis*, 6th ed. New York: McGraw Hill Book Company, 1964.

Sanford, Carol. "A Self-Organizing Leadership View of Paradigms," In *New Traditions in Business: Spirit and Leadership in the 21st Century*, ed. John Renesch. San Francisco: Berrett-Koehler Publishers, 1992.

Sanger, David E. and Steve Lohr. "The Downsizing of America, Is There a Better Way? A Search for Answers," *New York Times*, 9 March 1996.

"Saturn, Lexus Customers Found to Be Most Satisfied in Survey," *Investor's Business Daily*, 14 June 1996.

Sawhill, John C. "The Tangled Web We Weave," *Nature Conservancy*, May/June 1992.

Schumacher, E. F. *Small Is Beautiful.* London: Blond and Briggs Ltd., 1973.

The Secret Teachings of Jesus: Four Gnostic Gospels. Translated, with an Introduction and Notes by Marvin W. Meyer. New York: Random House, 1984.

"Share the Work," *Investor's Business Daily*, 6 June 1997.

Shellenbarger, Sue. "Work & Family," *Wall Street Journal*, 1 March 1995.

Sherman, Stratford. "Secrets of HP's 'Muddled' Team," *Fortune*, 18 March 1996.

Simon, Virginia. "A Commitment to the Earth," *Target Marketing*, January 1993.

Singer, June. *Androgyny: Toward a New Theory of Sexuality.* Garden City, NY: Anchor Press/Doubleday, 1976.

Smith, Adam. *An Inquiry into the Nature and Causes of the Wealth of Nations.* Edited with an introduction and commentary by Kathryn Sutherland. World Classics. Oxford: Oxford University Press, 1993.

Smith, Huston. *Forgotten Truth: The Common Vision of the World's Religions.* New York: HarperCollins, 1992.

Sperry, Paul. "Corporate Bulimia," *Investor's Business Daily*, 9 April 1996.

Strock, Gail. "Walnut Acres a Major Player in Organic Foods Industry," *Pennsylvania Business Central*, 26 May–8 June 1995.

Sugarman, Carole. "Keeping the Faith at Walnut Acres," *Washington Post*, 7 August 1991.

Talbot, Michael. *The Holographic Universe.* New York: HarperCollins, 1991.

Targ, Russell and Keith Harary. *The Mind Race: Understanding and Using Psychic Abilities.* With a Foreword by Willis Harman. New York: Villard Books, 1984.

Tart, Charles T. *Waking Up: Overcoming the Obstacles to Human Potential.* New Science Library. Boston: Shambhala Publications, 1986.

Three Initiates. *The Kybalion.* Chicago: The Yogi Publication Society, 1912.

"Time with Kids More Important than Money," *Investor's Business Daily*, 11 June 1996.

Weil, Andrew, M.D. *Spontaneous Healing.* New York: Alfred A. Knopf, 1995.

Wesemann, Carl. "The Primary Energy Source, or, Food for Thought." In *Energy Sources 78/79.* Edited by Rita Blome. Denver: ENERCOM, 1978.

"When It Comes to Service, General Motors Tops All," *Investor's Business Daily*, 28 May 1997.

White, John. *What Is Enlightenment?* Los Angeles: Jeremy P. Tarcher, 1985.

Wicks, Judy. "Women Changing Business," *Philadelphia Inquirer*, 6 March 1995.

Wilber, Ken. *Up from Eden: A Transpersonal View of Human Evolution.* Boulder, CO: Shambhala Publications, 1983.

Winner, Anna Kennedy. *The Basic Ideas of Occult Wisdom.* Wheaton, IL: The Theosophical Publishing House, 1970.

Wolpert, Stanley. *India.* Berkeley, CA: University of California Press, 1991.

Women: The New Providers. New York: Families and Work Institute, 1995.

Woodruff, David. "Women Lead the Pack in East German Startups," *Business Week*, 6 June 1996.

Yearning for Balance. Prepared for the Merck Family Fund by The Harwood Group, July 1995.

Yogananda, Paramahansa. *Autobiography of a Yogi.* Los Angeles: Self-Realization Fellowship, 1983.

_____. *The Law of Success*, 7th ed. Los Angeles: Self-Realization Fellowship, 1983.

_____. *Scientific Healing Affirmations.* Los Angeles: Self-Realization Fellowship, 1981.

Zackary, Pascal G. "Worried Workers," *Wall Street Journal*, 8 June 1995.

Zukav, Gary. "Evolution and Business." In *The New Paradigm in Business: Emerging Strategies for Leadership and Organizational Change*, edited by Michael Ray and Alan Rinzler. New York: Putnam Publishing Group for the World Business Academy, 1993.

_____. *The Seat of the Soul.* A Fireside Book. New York: Simon & Schuster, 1989.

Index

Page numbers in *italics* denote figures; "t" denotes tables

Butterworth–Heinemann Business Books . . .
for Transforming Business

Leading Consciously: A Pilgrimage Toward Self Mastery,
    Debashis Chatterjee, 0-7506-9864-0

Leading from the Heart: Choosing Courage over Fear in the Workplace,
    Kay Gilley, 0-7506-9835-7

Learning to Read the Signs: Reclaiming Pragmatism in Business,
    F. Byron Nahser, 0-7506-9901-9

Leveraging People and Profit: The Hard Work of Soft Management,
    Bernard A. Nagle and Perry Pascarella, 0-7506-9961-2

Marketing Plans That Work: Targeting Growth and Profitability,
    Malcolm H.B. McDonald and Warren J. Keegan, 0-7506-9828-4

A Place to Shine: Emerging from the Shadows at Work,
    Daniel S. Hanson, 0-7506-9738-5

Power Partnering: A Strategy for Business Excellence in the 21st Century,
    Sean Gadman, 0-7506-9809-8

Putting Emotional Intelligence to Work: Successful Leadership is More Than IQ,
    David Ryback, 0-7506-9956-6

Resources for the Knowledge-Based Economy Series

   The Knowledge Economy,
       Dale Neef, 0-7506-9936-1

   Knowledge Management and Organizational Design,
       Paul S. Myers, 0-7506-9749-0

   Knowledge Management Tools,
       Rudy L. Ruggles, III, 0-7506-9849-7

   Knowledge in Organizations,
       Laurence Prusak, 0-7506-9718-0

   The Strategic Management of Intellectual Capital,
       David A. Klein, 0-7506-9850-0

The Rhythm of Business: The Key to Building and Running Successful Companies,
    Jeffrey C. Shuman, 0-7506-9991-4

Setting the PACE® in Product Development: A Guide to Product And Cycle-time Excellence,
    Michael E. McGrath, 0-7506-9789-X

Time to Take Control: The Impact of Change on Corporate Computer Systems,
    Tony Johnson, 0-7506-9863-2

The Transformation of Management,
    Mike Davidson, 0-7506-9814-4

What Is the Emperor Wearing? Truth-Telling in Business Relationships,
    Laurie Weiss, 0-7506-9872-1

Who We Could Be at Work, Revised Edition,
    Margaret A. Lulic, 0-7506-9739-3

Working from Your Core: Personal and Corporate Wisdom in a World of Change,
    Sharon Seivert, 0-7506-9931-0

To purchase any Butterworth–Heinemann title,
please visit your local bookstore or call 1-800-366-2665.

About the Author

David A. Schwerin has over thirty years of business experience, the last twenty-two as President of D J Investment Advisors, Inc. He has an MBA in Finance, a Ph.D. in Religious Studies, and has taught economics on the college level. David has given expert witness testimony, has had numerous articles published, and has been widely quoted in the press. Most recently, he has contributed to the anthology, *The New Bottom Line: Bringing Heart and Soul to Business.*

As a student of the Perennial Philosophy for more than thirty years, David sees the teachings of ageless wisdom forming a foundation for many of the transformative shifts taking hold in the world of business and presents workshops on related topics. A member of the Financial Analysts Federation and a director of Spiritual Frontiers Fellowship International, David resides in the Philadelphia suburbs and can be reached at:

P.O. Box 754
Spring House, PA 19477
e-mail: schwerin@erols.com